TRANSMATH™
Understanding Algebraic Expressions

Interactive Text

John Woodward
Mary Stroh

Cambium
LEARNING®

BOSTON, MA | LONGMONT, CO

11 12 13 14 15   B&B   16 15 14 13 12

ISBN 13: 978-160697-045-4
ISBN: 1-60697-045-3

182001/7-12

Printed in the United States of America
Published and distributed by

Cambium
LEARNING®
Sopris West®

4093 Specialty Place • Longmont, CO 80504 • (303) 651-2829
www.voyagerlearning.com

TABLE OF CONTENTS

Name _____ Date _____

Skills Maintenance
Multiplication Facts and Extended Facts

Activity 1

Complete the multiplication facts and extended facts.

1. $3 \cdot 4 = $ _____

2. _____ $\cdot 7 = 35$

3. $50 \cdot $ _____ $= 350$

4. $3 \cdot 40 = $ _____

5. $8 \cdot 2 = $ _____

6. _____ $\cdot 2 = 160$

7. $1{,}600 = $ _____ $\cdot 200$

8. _____ $\cdot 5 = 3{,}500$

9. $8 \cdot 6 = $ _____

10. $80 \cdot $ _____ $= 480$

11. _____ $\cdot 600 = 4{,}800$

12. $9 \cdot $ _____ $= 63$

13. $630 = $ _____ $\cdot 90$

14. $4 \cdot 6 = $ _____

15. $40 \cdot 6 = $ _____

16. $4 \cdot 600 = $ _____

Name _____ Date _____

%÷ Apply Skills
=< x Fair Shares and Operations on Fractions

Activity 1

Add or subtract the fractions.

1. $\frac{3}{5} + \frac{2}{5}$ _____

2. $\frac{4}{9} - \frac{1}{9}$ _____

3. $\frac{5}{7} + \frac{1}{7}$ _____

4. $\frac{8}{7} - \frac{1}{7}$ _____

5. $\frac{12}{10} + \frac{3}{10}$ _____

6. $\frac{22}{9} - \frac{20}{9}$ _____

Activity 2

Divide each of the shapes into fair shares and shade the part to match the given fraction.

1. $\frac{1}{4}$

2. $\frac{2}{3}$

3. $\frac{5}{5}$

4. $\frac{1}{2}$

5. $\frac{4}{6}$

Name _____ Date _____

Problem-Solving Activity
Organizing Data

The local movie theater has to keep track of how much money it makes so that it stays in business. The table shows data from one week of sales for the Lakewood Cineplex. It shows the amount of each item sold for every day of the week. For example, the theater sold 200 adult tickets on Monday night. They also sold 75 bags of popcorn. Answer the questions based on the table. You may use a calculator.

	Monday	Tuesday	Wednesday	Thursday	Friday	Saturday	Sunday
adult	200	120	150	219	306	390	225
child	39	47	35	52	120	250	87
popcorn	75	82	93	72	151	216	193
sodas	78	4	86	94	243	217	188
candy	90	83	86	92	142	168	95

1. What was the average number of popcorn sales for the week? What was the average number of soda sales? _____

2. What was the average number of adult tickets sold? What was the average number of child tickets sold? _____

3. Look at the patterns in the adult and child tickets. Explain why you think there is such a difference in the average number of tickets for adults and children.

   _____

   _____

4. Which day did the soda machine break? Use the minimum to explain your answer.

   _____

   _____

mBook Reinforce Understanding
Use the mBook *Study Guide* to review lesson concepts.

Name _____ Date _____

 Skills Maintenance
Adding and Subtracting Fractions

Activity 1

Add or subtract the fractions.

1. $\frac{3}{5} + \frac{2}{5}$ _____

2. $\frac{4}{9} - \frac{3}{9}$ _____

3. $\frac{7}{8} + \frac{10}{8}$ _____

4. $\frac{3}{7} + \frac{1}{7}$ _____

5. $\frac{22}{4} - \frac{15}{4}$ _____

6. $\frac{15}{10} + \frac{10}{10}$ _____

Ordering Statistics

Activity 2

Tell the maximum, minimum, range, mode, and mean.

1. The data set is 40   20   60   80   50   20

   Max _____   Min _____

   Range _____   Mode _____   Mean _____

2. The data set is 20   4   1   10   3   7   2   8   9   6   7

   Max _____   Min _____

   Range _____   Mode _____   Mean _____

Name _____ Date _____

 Apply Skills
Equivalent Fractions

Activity 1

Find the least common denominator (LCD) using tables of multiples.
Circle the LCD, then solve the problem.

1. $\frac{1}{5} + \frac{1}{4}$ _____ The table of multiples is:

4	4	8	12	16	20	24
5	5	10	15	20	25	30

2. $\frac{1}{2} - \frac{1}{3}$ _____ Fill in the table of multiples.

2					
3					

Activity 2

Fill in a fraction equal to 1 to find the equivalent fraction with the LCD
for each number. Then solve the problem.

1. $\frac{1}{4} + \frac{2}{3}$

   The LCD is 12. Change the fractions to equivalent fractions with the LCD of 12.

   $\frac{1}{4} \cdot \boxed{1 \frac{}{}} = \frac{}{12}$ $\frac{2}{3} \cdot \boxed{1 \frac{}{}} = \frac{}{12}$

   Rewrite the problem. _____ Answer _____

2. $\frac{2}{3} - \frac{1}{9}$

   The LCD is 9. Change the fractions to equivalent fractions with the LCD of 9.

   $\frac{2}{3} \cdot \boxed{1 \frac{}{}} = \frac{}{9}$ $\frac{1}{9} \cdot \boxed{1 \frac{}{}} = \frac{}{9}$

   Rewrite the problem. _____ Answer _____

Name _____ Date _____

 ### Skills Maintenance
Adding and Subtracting Fractions

Activity 1

Find the LCD, then add or subtract the fractions.

1. $\frac{3}{5} + \frac{2}{8}$ _____

2. $\frac{7}{6} - \frac{2}{3}$ _____

3. $\frac{1}{8} + \frac{7}{8}$ _____

4. $\frac{1}{6} - \frac{1}{9}$ _____

Name _____ Date _____

 Apply Skills
Multiplying Fractions

Activity 1

Select the area model that shows the answer to each of the problems.
Circle your answer.

1. $\frac{1}{4} \cdot \frac{4}{5} = \frac{4}{20}$

(a)

(b)

(c)

2. $\frac{1}{2} \cdot \frac{4}{5} = \frac{4}{10}$

(a)

(b)

(c)

3. $\frac{1}{3} \cdot \frac{6}{7} = \frac{6}{21}$

(a)

(b)

(c)

Activity 2

Tell what problem matches the area model.

1.

(a) $\frac{2}{3} \cdot \frac{3}{4} = \frac{6}{12}$

(b) $\frac{1}{3} \cdot \frac{2}{3} = \frac{2}{9}$

(c) $\frac{1}{2} \cdot \frac{2}{3} = \frac{2}{6}$

2.

(a) $\frac{2}{3} \cdot \frac{3}{4} = \frac{6}{12}$

(b) $\frac{1}{3} \cdot \frac{2}{3} = \frac{2}{9}$

(c) $\frac{1}{2} \cdot \frac{2}{3} = \frac{2}{6}$

3.

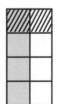

(a) $\frac{2}{4} \cdot \frac{2}{4} = \frac{4}{16}$

(b) $\frac{3}{4} \cdot \frac{1}{2} = \frac{3}{8}$

(c) $\frac{1}{4} \cdot \frac{1}{2} = \frac{1}{8}$

Name _____ Date _____

Problem-Solving Activity
More on Statistics

Take a survey of your class to see how many times in the past month people have eaten a certain food. Create both a tally chart and an ordered list in the space below. Then compute the median and the mean for the data set. Write a few sentences describing the difference between the median and the mean.

_____

_____

_____

_____

_____

_____

mBook Reinforce Understanding
Use the mBook *Study Guide* to review lesson concepts.

Name _____ Date _____

Skills Maintenance
Adding and Subtracting Fractions

Activity 1

Add and subtract the fractions.

1. $\frac{2}{3} + \frac{1}{6}$ _____

2. $\frac{4}{5} - \frac{1}{3}$ _____

3. $\frac{3}{4} + \frac{5}{6}$ _____

4. $\frac{8}{9} - \frac{1}{2}$ _____

Statistics

Activity 2

Rewrite the data sets in order. Then tell the maximum, minimum, range, and median.

1. Data Set: 3, 5, 1, 2, 4, 8, and 9

   Rewrite _____

   Max _____   Min _____

   Range _____   Median _____

2. Data Set: 4, 3, 7, 10, and 5

   Rewrite _____

   Max _____   Min _____

   Range _____   Median _____

3. Data Set: 4, 2, 12, 8, 2, and 1

   Rewrite _____

   Max _____   Min _____

   Range _____   Median _____

Name _____ Date _____

Apply Skills
Multiply and Simplify

Activity 1

Multiply across to solve the problems. Then simplify the answer.

1. $\frac{2}{3} \cdot \frac{3}{5} =$ _____
    Simplify.

    _____ = 1— • _____

2. $\frac{4}{6} \cdot \frac{1}{2} =$ _____
    Simplify.

    _____ = 1— • _____

3. $\frac{3}{4} \cdot \frac{2}{8} =$ _____
    Simplify.

    _____ = 1— • _____

Name _____ Date _____

 Problem-Solving Activity
Putting It All Together

Kari is trying to get in shape for the track team at her high school. She wants to be a distance runner, so she has been trying to run every day. Her goal is to run about 50 miles each week. Use what you learned about the minimum, maximum, mean, and median to answer the questions.

	Week 1	Week 2	Week 3
Monday	7	18	6
Tuesday	2	20	9
Wednesday	8	2	8
Thursday	6	1	9
Friday	8	0	8
Saturday	6	0	7
Sunday	12	1	9

1. Fill in the table.

	Week 1	Week 2	Week 3
Min			
Max			
Mean			
Median			

2. During Week 2, Kari injured herself by trying to run too much at the beginning of the week. Describe how the data show that the mean number of miles for the week is not a good indicator of how much she ran each day. Use the minimum, maximum, and median to explain your thinking.

_____

_____

_____

_____

 Reinforce Understanding
Use the mBook *Study Guide* to review lesson concepts.

Name _____ Date _____

 ## Skills Maintenance
Multiplying Fractions

Activity 1

Multiply across and simplify your answers.

1. $\frac{3}{4} \cdot \frac{1}{3}$ _____

   Simplify _____

2. $\frac{4}{8} \cdot \frac{1}{2}$ _____

   Simplify _____

3. $\frac{4}{6} \cdot \frac{3}{4}$ _____

   Simplify _____

Statistics

Activity 2

Find the statistics for each data set.

1. Data Set: 1, 2, 2, 3, 4, 5, 6, 8, 9

Max _____   Min _____

Mode _____   Range _____   Median _____

2. Data Set: 3, 7, 9, 9, 9, 10, 12

Max _____   Min _____

Mode _____   Range _____   Median _____

3. Data Set: 5, 8, 10, 14

Max _____   Min _____

Mode _____   Range _____   Median _____

Name _____ Date _____

Apply Skills
Dividing Fractions

Activity 1

Tell what the unit is and how many units are needed to divide the number on a number line. Then solve the problem.

1. $\dfrac{5}{8} \div \dfrac{1}{8}$

The unit is _____ and you need _____ of them. $\dfrac{5}{8} \div \dfrac{1}{8}$ _____

2. $\dfrac{4}{3} \div \dfrac{1}{3}$

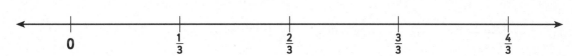

The unit is _____ and you need _____ of them. $\dfrac{4}{3} \div \dfrac{1}{3}$ _____

Activity 2

Divide by inverting and multiplying. Simplify the answer.

1. $\dfrac{3}{5} \div \dfrac{1}{5}$ _____ • _____ = _____ Simplify _____

2. $\dfrac{1}{8} \div \dfrac{1}{6}$ _____ • _____ = _____ Simplify _____

3. $2 \div \dfrac{1}{2}$ _____ • _____ = _____ Simplify _____

mBook Reinforce Understanding
Use the mBook *Study Guide* to review lesson concepts.

Name _____ Date _____

Skills Maintenance
Multiplying and Dividing Fractions

Activity 1

Multiply. Simplify the answers if necessary.

1. $\frac{4}{5} \cdot \frac{2}{3}$ _____   Simplify _____

2. $\frac{3}{9} \cdot \frac{1}{3}$ _____   Simplify _____

3. $\frac{6}{8} \cdot \frac{1}{10}$ _____   Simplify _____

Activity 2

Divide using invert and multiply. Simplify the answers.

1. $\frac{4}{5} \div \frac{1}{5}$ _____ • _____ = _____   Simplify _____

2. $6 \div \frac{1}{2}$ _____ • _____ = _____   Simplify _____

3. $\frac{3}{8} \div \frac{1}{4}$ _____ • _____ = _____   Simplify _____

Name _____ Date _____

Apply Skills
Mixed Practice With Fractions

Activity 1

Look at the mix of fraction problems. Think carefully about the correct strategy before you start each problem and write a short explanation of the strategy. Then solve the problem. Simplify answers when necessary.

1. $\frac{4}{7} \div \frac{1}{7}$ The strategy for division is:

_____

Solve _____

2. $\frac{8}{9} + \frac{1}{6}$ The strategy for addition is:

_____

Solve _____

3. $\frac{3}{4} - \frac{1}{2}$ The strategy for subtraction is:

_____

Solve _____

4. $\frac{3}{5} \cdot \frac{2}{3}$ The strategy for multiplication is:

_____

Solve _____

Activity 2

Fill in the missing numbers in the problems involving reciprocals.

1. $\frac{3}{5} \cdot$ _____ $= 1$ 2. $\frac{4}{5} \cdot \frac{5}{4} =$ _____   3. _____ $\cdot \frac{2}{1} = 1$

4. $6 \cdot$ _____ $= 1$ 5. $\frac{8}{9} \cdot \frac{9}{8} =$ _____   6. _____ $\cdot 7 = 1$

7. $\frac{1}{8} \cdot$ _____ $= 1$ 8. $\frac{1}{3} \cdot \frac{3}{1} =$ _____   9. _____ $\cdot \frac{10}{1} = 1$

Name _____ Date _____

Problem-Solving Activity
Box-and-Whisker Plots

The data shows the times in seconds for all students in the 200-yard dash. Use the data to make a box-and-whisker plot next to the table. Then answer the questions. Make sure to identify where the median and halfway point in the range are.

Seth	40
Marcus	41
Paige	50
Robert	53
Tracey	55
Oscar	55
Michael	57
Joshua	59
Amber	60
Erica	60
Ryan	61
Brittany	62
DeAnne	62
Lamar	62
Autumn	63

1. What are the mean and the overall median for this set of data?

    _____

2. Describe the difference between the way those in the bottom $\frac{1}{4}$ are grouped than those in the top $\frac{1}{4}$.

    _____

3. Which of these students has a more extreme time for the 200—DeAnne or Marcus? Explain why, using the box-and-whisker plot.

    _____

    _____

mBook Reinforce Understanding
Use the mBook *Study Guide* to review lesson concepts.

Name _____ Date _____

 Skills Maintenance
Fraction Operations

Activity 1

Solve the mix of fraction operations. Remember to look carefully to determine the correct strategy. Simplify the answers if necessary.

1. $\frac{3}{5} + \frac{2}{9}$ _____ Simplify _____

2. $\frac{4}{8} \cdot \frac{3}{5}$ _____ Simplify _____

3. $\frac{5}{6} \cdot \frac{2}{3}$ _____ Simplify _____

4. $\frac{5}{7} \div \frac{1}{7}$ _____ Simplify _____

5. $\frac{2}{3} - \frac{1}{4}$ _____ Simplify _____

6. $\frac{2}{3} \div \frac{1}{2}$ _____ Simplify _____

Name _____ Date _____

 Apply Skills
Decimal Numbers

Activity 1

Place an X on the number line in the approximate location of each of the decimal numbers. Then explain why you chose the location.

1. Where would you find 0.78?

Explain _____

_____

_____

2. Where would you find 0.10?

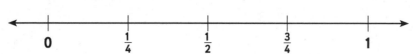

Explain _____

_____

_____

Activity 2

Convert the fractions to decimal numbers and decimal numbers to fractions. If needed, you may use a calculator.

1. $\frac{3}{5}$ = _____

2. _____ = 0.10

3. $\frac{1}{4}$ = _____

4. $\frac{5}{6}$ = _____

5. _____ = 0.75

6. _____ = 0.33

Problem-Solving Activity
Drawing Box-and-Whisker Plots

Isabel Martinez is the Assistant Principal at Viega Middle School. She is looking over attendance data. She is particularly interested in one class where a number of students are absent on a regular basis. The table shows a list of data for the class and the number of days that students were absent for September, October, and November. Use this information and the box-and-whisker plot to answer the questions.

Student Name	Number of Days Absent
Amelia	3
Juan	0
Carmen	20
Sara	6
Luisa	2
Malena	22
Hector	2
Jessica	4
Eva	1
Pedro	1
James	3
Julie	4
Violeta	2
Carlos	2
Marshall	5
Cristina	24
Rena	3
Cyndie	2
Michael	0
Adam	4
Alberto	2
Cara	6
Jennifer	3
Mica	4
Jana	5

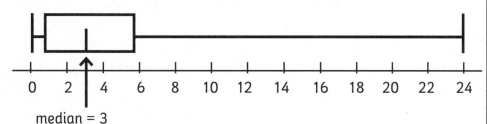

median = 3

1. Is Mica absent a typical amount of time? Explain your thinking using the box-and-whisker plot.

   _____

   _____

2. Carlos thinks he has a much better attendance rate than the rest of the students in his class. He has only been absent two times in the first three months. He tells his teacher this, but she says, "No, you've missed about the same amount as everyone else." Explain why the teacher is right using the box-and-whisker plot.

   _____

   _____

3. What three students should the assistant principal bring into her office? Explain why.

   _____

   _____

   _____

mBook Reinforce Understanding
Use the mBook *Study Guide* to review lesson concepts.

Name _____ Date _____

 Skills Maintenance
Converting Fractions and Decimal Numbers

Activity 1

Convert the fractions to decimal numbers. You should be able to do these conversions without a calculator.

1. $\dfrac{3}{4}$ _____

2. $\dfrac{1}{2}$ _____

3. $\dfrac{9}{4}$ _____

4. $\dfrac{3}{2}$ _____

5. $\dfrac{1}{3}$ _____

Activity 2

Convert the decimal numbers to fractions without using a calculator.

1. 0.4 _____

2. 0.25 _____

3. 0.5 _____

4. 0.17 _____

5. 0.01 _____

6. 0.99 _____

Name _____ Date _____

 Apply Skills
Working With Decimal Numbers

Activity 1

Round the decimal numbers.

1. 0.251

    Rounded to the tenths place _____

    Rounded to the hundredths place _____

2. 0.083

    Rounded to the tenths place _____

    Rounded to the hundredths place _____

3. 0.115

    Rounded to the tenths place _____

    Rounded to the hundredths place _____

4. 0.378

    Rounded to the tenths place _____

    Rounded to the hundredths place _____

Activity 2

Use a calculator to convert the fractions to decimal numbers. Write the repeating decimal numbers using the repeat sign over the top of the repeating part.

1. $\frac{5}{11}$ _____

2. $\frac{1}{7}$ _____

3. $\frac{5}{6}$ _____

4. $\frac{8}{9}$ _____

5. $\frac{2}{3}$ _____

Name _____ Date _____

Problem-Solving Activity
Interpreting Box-and-Whisker Plots

The table shows weights of wrestlers on a high school team. Fill in the necessary information on the box-and-whisker plot, then use the information to answer the questions.

Wrestler	Weight	
Eric	68	bottom $\frac{1}{4}$
Brad	74	
Corey	98	
Sam	104	
Angelo	110	middle $\frac{1}{2}$
Lee	132	
Reggie	135	
Ryan	142	
Herky	142	
Kevin	144	
Donte	148	
Jason	182	
Michael	187	top $\frac{1}{4}$
Josh	189	
Dwayne	193	
Larry	194	

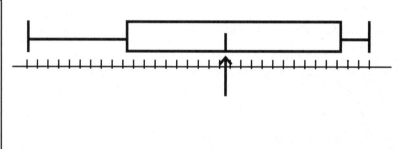

1. Begin by computing the mean and median. What is the difference between the mean and the median?

   _____

2. Is the median closer to 68 or 194?

   _____

3. Describe how Josh and Brad wrestle in different categories (lightweight vs. heavyweight) based on the box-and-whisker plot.

   _____

4. What do you notice that is different about wrestlers in the bottom $\frac{1}{4}$ of the box-and-whisker plot and those in the top $\frac{1}{4}$?

   _____

Name _____ Date _____

 Skills Maintenance
Rounding Decimal Numbers

Activity 1

Round the decimal numbers to the nearest tenths place.

1. 0.25 _____

2. 0.058 _____

3. 0.519 _____

Activity 2

Round the decimal numbers to the nearest hundredths place.

1. 0.011 _____

2. 0.202 _____

3. 0.375 _____

Activity 3

Rewrite the repeating decimal numbers using the repeat sign.

Model	$\frac{4}{11}$ = 0.3636363636363636363 Answer: 0.$\overline{36}$

1. $\frac{5}{9}$ = 0.5555555555555555 _____

2. $\frac{1}{11}$ = 0.0909090909090909 _____

3. $\frac{58}{7}$ = 8.285714285714285 _____

4. $\frac{35}{11}$ = 3.18181818181818 _____

Name _____   Date _____

Apply Skills
Adding and Subtracting Decimal Numbers

Activity 1

Add and subtract. Line up the numbers in the boxes provided. Check your answers by rounding to the nearest whole numbers.

1. 44.05 − 27.18

    Answer _____

    Check Your Answer _____

    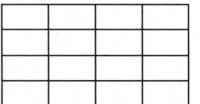

2. 42.01 + 9.8 + 27.001

    Answer _____

    Check Your Answer _____

    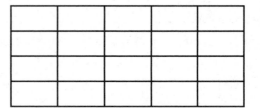

3. 103.81 − 86.021

    Answer _____

    Check Your Answer _____

    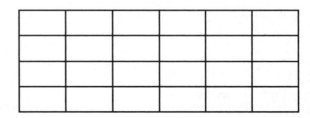

Activity 2

Round to the nearest whole number, then add.

1. 23.7 + 14.8   Round _____   Estimate _____

2. 45.8 − 19.7   Round _____   Estimate _____

3. 5.8 + 2.7   Round _____   Estimate _____

4. 128.01 − 39.17   Round _____   Estimate _____

5. 198.7 + 229.6   Round _____   Estimate _____

6. 729.5 − 436.89   Round _____   Estimate _____

Name _____ Date _____

 Problem-Solving Activity
Scatter Plots

The police in Jefferson County are concerned about speeding on Highway 601. They want to see if there is a pattern in the number of speeding tickets that they give out and the time of day. Plot the data from the table in the scatter plot and answer the questions.

Time of Day	Number of Speeding Tickets
7 a.m.	25
8 a.m.	24
9 a.m.	35
10 a.m.	15
11 a.m.	17
12 p.m.	40
1 p.m.	9
2 p.m.	18
3 p.m.	32
4 p.m.	17
5 p.m.	25
6 p.m.	38

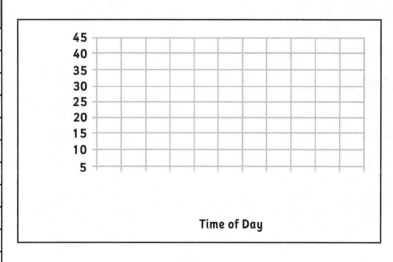

Based on the data in the scatter plot, do you think there is a pattern to the speeding during the day on Highway 601? Use the points in the scatter plot to explain your thinking.

_____

_____

_____

_____

mBook **Reinforce Understanding**
Use the mBook *Study Guide* to review lesson concepts.

Name _____ Date _____

Skills Maintenance
Adding and Subtracting Decimal Numbers

Activity 1

Line up the problems to add or subtract, then check your work by rounding.

1. 22.7 + 88.95 _____
2. 37.09 − 25.79 _____
3. 188.75 + 122.9 _____
4. 107.12 − 98.9 _____

Relationships in Scatter Plots

Activity 2

Tell if there is a relationship between the variables in the scatter plots. Circle the correct answer.

1.
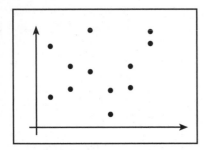

Relationship   or   No Relationship

2.
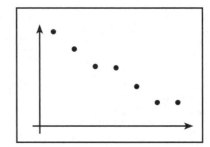

Relationship   or   No Relationship

3.
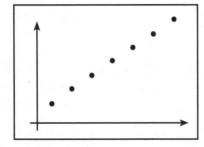

Relationship   or   No Relationship

4.
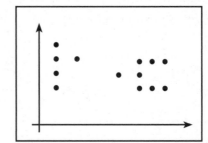

Relationship   or   No Relationship

Name _____ Date _____

 Apply Skills
Comparing Decimal Numbers

Activity 1

Use the decimal ruler to put the decimal numbers in order.

1. 0.9, 0.09, 0.1, 0.07

   In order from smallest to largest _____

2. 1.2, 1.05, 1.5, 1.005

   In order from smallest to largest _____

3. 2.7, 2.05, 2.75, 2.07

   In order from smallest to largest _____

4. 0.3, 0.08, 0.003, 0.83

   In order from smallest to largest _____

Activity 2

Match the decimal number with its approximate location on the number line.

0.52   0.25   0.75   0.620   0.062

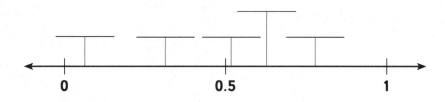

mBook Reinforce Understanding
Use the mBook *Study Guide* to review lesson concepts.

Name _____ Date _____

Skills Maintenance
Decimal Numbers

Activity 1

Add or subtract the decimal numbers. Round your answers to the nearest tenths place.

1.   2.37 + 4.8 + 1.778 _____

2.   107.04 − 33.3 _____

3.   47.29 + 33.87 + 29.76 _____

4.   5,001.01 − 4,999.9 _____

5.   527.8 + 395.769 _____

Activity 2

Put the decimal numbers in order from smallest to largest.

1.   2.03, 0.032, 3.20 _____

2.   0.09, 0.1, 0.8 _____

3.   4.72, 4.07, 4.2 _____

4.   5.11, 1.51, 0.151 _____

5.   0.01, 0.2, 0.009 _____

Name _____ Date _____

%÷ Apply Skills
Multiplication of Decimal Numbers

Activity 1

Use the 100-square grid to help you solve the problems.

1. 0.10 · 0.20 _____

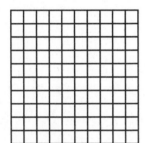

2. 0.5 · 0.6 _____

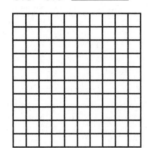

3. 0.70 · 0.10 _____

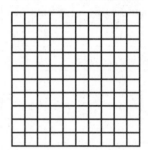

Activity 2

Select the problem represented by each of the 100-square grids below.

1.

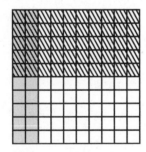

   (a) 0.20 · 0.05 = 0.01

   (b) 0.20 · 0.50 = 0.10

   (c) 0.02 · 0.05 = 0.001

2.

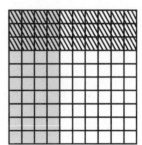

   (a) 0.4 · 0.3 = 0.12

   (b) 0.4 · 0.03 = 0.012

   (c) 0.004 · 0.3 = 0.0012

3.

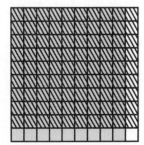

   (a) 0.09 · 0.9 = 0.081

   (b) 0.90 · 0.10 = 0.09

   (c) 0.90 · 0.90 = 0.81

4.

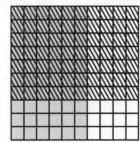

   (a) 0.6 · 0.07 = 0.042

   (b) 0.6 · 0.7 = 0.42

   (c) 0.06 · 0.7 = 0.042

Name _____ Date _____

Problem-Solving Activity
Direct Relationships

Create a scatter plot from the data in the table. After you have made your scatter plot, answer the questions.

Number of Bounces	Height of the Ball (in)
1	72
2	60
3	55
4	40
5	35
6	30
7	20
8	10
9	3
10	1

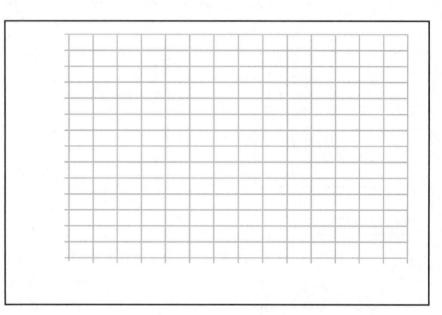

1. Is there a relationship between the height of the ball and the number of bounces? Verify your answer with examples from the data.

   _____

   _____

2. Is the relationship a direct relationship? Explain.

   _____

   _____

3. In your own words, describe a direct relationship and how you can tell whether or not a scatter plot represents a direct relationship.

   _____

   _____

   _____

Name _____ Date _____

 Skills Maintenance
Multiplying Decimal Numbers

Activity 1

Use the 100-square grid to multiply.

1. $0.30 \cdot 0.50$ _____

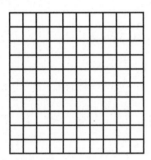

2. $0.70 \cdot 0.2$ _____

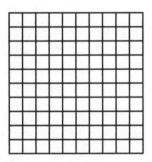

3. $0.80 \cdot 0.70$ _____

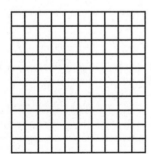

Name _____ Date _____

 Apply Skills
Traditional Multiplication of Decimal Numbers and Number Sense

> **Activity 1**

Circle the correct answer to each of the problems.

1. 0.3 · 0.21   0.063   0.63   6.3   2. 0.05 · 0.1   0.005   0.05   0.5

3. 0.002 · 0.7   0.0014   0.014   0.14   4. 0.8 · 0.9   0.0072   0.072   0.72

5. 0.6 · 0.04   0.0024   0.024   0.24   6. 4 · 0.25   0.01   0.10   1.00

> **Activity 2**

Multiply the decimal numbers using the traditional method. Check your answers using rounding strategies.

1. 0.85 · 0.8 _____

    Check _____

    _____

2. 5.3 · 2.5 _____

    Check _____

    _____

3. 0.49 · 2.6 _____

    Check _____

    _____

4. 12.01 · 0.23 _____

    Check _____

    _____

5. 0.5 · 36.4 _____

    Check _____

Name _____ Date _____

Problem-Solving Activity
Indirect Relationships

Psychologists have studied people's memory for a long time. One of the experiments they have done is to have people memorize pairs of words. The words in each pair don't go together, so it is hard to find an easy way to remember them. For example, one pair might be "zebra—ocean." Generally, people can do a pretty good job remembering the pairs right away, but as time goes by, they remember less and less. Perform the experiement in pairs and record the data in the table. Then plot the dots in the scatter plot. Identify the relationship in the scatter plot, and describe how you came to that conclusion.

_____

_____

_____

_____

_____

List of Word Pairs	Test 1	Test 2	Test 3	Test 4
computer—shark				
mountain—snow				
tall—river				
snake—zebra				
television—chair				
card—carrot				
whistle—sound				
work—study				

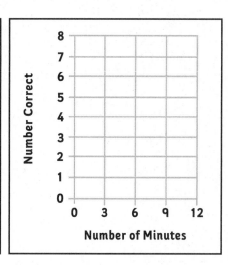

mBook Reinforce Understanding
Use the mBook *Study Guide* to review lesson concepts.

Name _____ Date _____

Skills Maintenance
Multiplying Decimal Numbers

Activity 1

Circle the correct answer.

1. $0.85 \cdot 0.7$ 0.0595   0.595   5.95

2. $0.2 \cdot 0.7$ 0.014   0.14   1.40

3. $6 \cdot 0.25$ 0.015   0.15   1.50

4. $0.03 \cdot 0.09$ 0.0027   0.027   0.27

Activity 2

Select the strategy for estimating the answer.

1. $0.25 \cdot 10$
   - (a) Think: $0.2 \cdot 0.1$
   - (b) Think: a quarter of 10
   - (c) Think: add a zero at the end

2. $8.4 \cdot 0.5$
   - (a) Think: $8 \cdot 0.5$
   - (b) Think: add a zero at the end
   - (c) Think: half of 8

3. $0.6 \cdot 0.1$
   - (a) Think: $6 \cdot 1 = 6$ and move the decimal over 2 places
   - (b) Think: six tenths minus one tenth
   - (c) Think: half of one

Name _____ Date _____

%÷ Apply Skills
≤ × Division of Decimal Numbers

Activity 1

Select the problem that is represented by the 100-square grid.

1.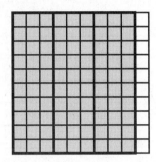

(a) 1.00 ÷ 0.3 = 0.3

(b) 0.9 ÷ 0.3 = 3

(c) 0.9 ÷ 0.3 = 0.3

2.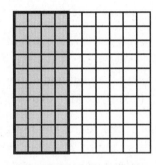

(a) 0.4 ÷ 0.2 = 2

(b) 0.4 ÷ 0.1 = 0.4

(c) 0.4 ÷ 0.4 = 1

3.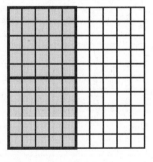

(a) 0.5 ÷ 0.25 = 2

(b) 0.5 ÷ 0.5 = 2

(c) 0.5 ÷ 0.25 = 0.2

4.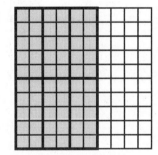

(a) 0.6 ÷ 0.3 = 3

(b) 0.6 ÷ 0.5 = 0.6

(c) 0.6 ÷ 0.1 = 6

Name _____ Date _____

 ## Problem-Solving Activity
The Line of Best Fit

It is especially difficult to read if the radio or TV is on. It gets worse when the sound is louder. This is a good example of an indirect relationship: The louder the sound, the worse (or lower) your ability to understand what you are reading.

The data in the table shows the results of an experiment. Students were given five minutes to read a short story. Then they were given 20 questions about the reading. The volume of the radio played at different levels from 0 (silent) to 10 (very loud).

The left column shows the volume of the radio. The right column shows the number of correct answers out of 20 questions. Use this table to complete the scatter plot and then create a line that best fits.

Volume of the Radio	Number of Correct Answers
0	18
0	17
1	15
1	16
2	14
2	13
3	13
3	14
4	11
4	13
5	10
6	9
6	8
7	5
7	4
8	4
8	3
9	3
10	3

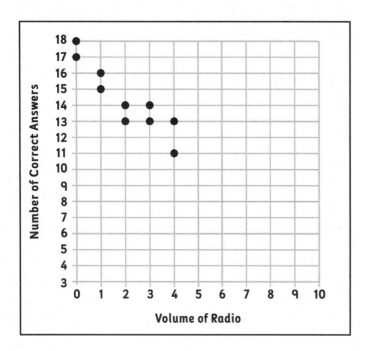

mBook Reinforce Understanding
Use the mBook *Study Guide* to review lesson concepts.

36   Unit 1 • Lesson 13

Name _____ Date _____

 Skills Maintenance
Understanding Division of Decimal Numbers

Activity 1

Answer the division problems using the 100-square grid.

1. $0.2 \div 0.1$ _____

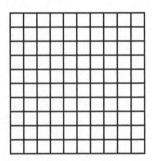

2. $0.6 \div 0.2$ _____

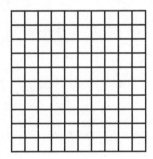

3. $1.00 \div 0.5$ _____

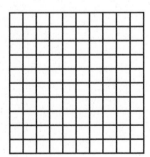

Name _____ Date _____

Apply Skills
The Traditional Method for Dividing Decimal Numbers

Activity 1

Place the decimal point in the correct location to complete the quotient for each problem. Use estimation to help you. Double-check your answers with a calculator.

1. $0.75 \div 3 = 0\ 2\ 5$

2. $7.5 \div 0.3 = 0\ 2\ 5$

3. $75 \div 3 = 0\ 2\ 5$

4. $0.8 \div 0.2 = 0\ 4\ 0$

5. $0.8 \div 2 = 0\ 4\ 0$

6. $0.50 \div 2 = 0\ 2\ 5$

7. $5 \div 2 = 0\ 2\ 5$

8. $0.3 \div 0.1 = 0\ 3\ 0$

9. $0.03 \div 1 = 0\ 3\ 0$

10. $0.3 \div 1 = 0\ 3\ 0$

Activity 2

Divide the problems using the traditional method. Check your work using rounding. Double-check your answers with a calculator.

1. $1.42 \div 0.5$ _____

2. $0.12 \div 0.59$ _____

3. $1.23 \div 0.4$ _____

4. $6.29 \div 0.2$ _____

5. $75.6 \div 7.2$ _____

6. $421.1 \div 59.7$ _____

Name _____ Date _____

Problem-Solving Activity
Choosing an Operation

Answer the questions based on the comic art.

Frame Width 1.4"

Frame Height 1.9"

Comic Strip Height 2.1"

1. Each frame has the same length and width. You can see the dimensions of a picture frame. What is the area of each frame?

   _____

2. Each frame is inside of a strip that has four frames and a border around each frame. The border is the same width all the way around. You can also see that the strip is 2.6" tall including two borders (one on top and one down below). How wide is a border?

   _____

3. How wide is the strip?

   _____

Name _____ Date _____

%÷ Skills Maintenance
Equivalent Fractions

Activity 1

Fill in a fraction equal to 1 to find the equivalent fraction with the LCD for each number. Then solve the problem.

1. $\frac{3}{4} + \frac{4}{6}$

The LCD is _____. Change the fractions to equivalent fractions with this LCD.

$\frac{3}{4} \cdot$ ⬜ $\dfrac{\ }{\ }$ = _____ $\frac{4}{6} \cdot$ ⬜ $\dfrac{\ }{\ }$ = _____

Rewrite the problem. _____   Answer _____

2. $\frac{2}{5} - \frac{3}{10}$

The LCD is _____. Change the fractions to equivalent fractions with this LCD.

$\frac{2}{5}$ ⬜ $\dfrac{\ }{\ }$ = _____ $\frac{3}{10}$ ⬜ $\dfrac{\ }{\ }$ = _____

Rewrite the problem. _____   Answer _____

Activity 2

Circle the simplified equivalent fraction for each.

1. $\frac{5}{10}$
   (a) $\frac{1}{5}$
   (b) $\frac{2}{10}$
   (c) $\frac{1}{2}$

2. $\frac{6}{18}$
   (a) $\frac{1}{2}$
   (b) $\frac{1}{3}$
   (c) $\frac{3}{9}$

3. $\frac{12}{15}$
   (a) $\frac{2}{12}$
   (b) $\frac{1}{15}$
   (c) $\frac{4}{5}$

4. $\frac{6}{24}$
   (a) $\frac{1}{4}$
   (b) $\frac{1}{6}$
   (c) $\frac{1}{3}$

5. $\frac{24}{32}$
   (a) $\frac{12}{16}$
   (b) $\frac{3}{4}$
   (c) $\frac{6}{8}$

Name _____ Date _____

Unit Review
Fractions and Decimal Numbers

Activity 1

Convert the decimal numbers to fractions and fractions to decimal numbers. Make sure your answers are in the simplest form.

1. 0.25 _____

2. $\frac{2}{6}$ _____

3. $\frac{1}{2}$ _____

4. $\frac{10}{7}$ _____

5. 0.6 _____

6. 0.9 _____

7. $\frac{15}{20}$ _____

8. 0.40 _____

Activity 2

Select the 100-square grid that best represents the problem.

1. 0.25 ÷ 0.05

  (a) 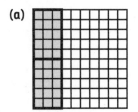   (b) 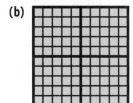   (c)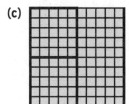

2. 1.00 ÷ 0.25

  (a) 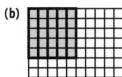   (b) 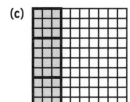   (c)

3. 0.4 ÷ 0.2

  (a) 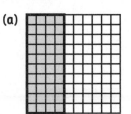   (b) 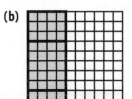   (c)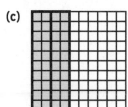

Name _____ Date _____

Activity 3

Add or subtract the fractions and decimal numbers. Simplify your answer.

1. $\dfrac{1}{2} + \dfrac{3}{6}$ _____

2. $\dfrac{1}{7} + \dfrac{5}{21}$ _____

3. $\dfrac{4}{5} - \dfrac{1}{3}$ _____

4. $0.90 - 0.45$ _____

5. $0.11 + 0.98$ _____

6. $\dfrac{8}{9} + \dfrac{1}{2}$ _____

7. $\dfrac{10}{20} - \dfrac{1}{4}$ _____

8. $0.06 + 0.60$ _____

9. $0.300 - 0.030$ _____

Activity 4

Multiply or divide the fractions and decimal numbers. Simplify your answer.

1. $0.5 \cdot 0.7$ _____   2. $\dfrac{1}{4} \cdot \dfrac{3}{7}$ _____

3. $\dfrac{3}{5} \div \dfrac{2}{5}$ _____   4. $\dfrac{3}{10} \cdot \dfrac{11}{3}$ _____

5. $\dfrac{1}{7} \cdot \dfrac{8}{9}$ _____   6. $0.2 \cdot 1.047$ _____

7. $0.9 \div 0.2$ _____   8. $0.004 \div 0.03$ _____

9. $\dfrac{7}{9} \div \dfrac{3}{6}$ _____

Name _____ Date _____

Unit Review
Statistics

Activity 1

Find the minimum, maximum, range, mean, and median for the data.

1. 1, 3, 3, 10, 11, 14, 26

Min _____ Max _____

Range _____ Mean _____ Median _____

2. 40, 5, 10, 9, 7, 33, 52, 12

Min _____ Max _____

Range _____ Mean _____ Median _____

Activity 2

Select the graphs that show a line of best fit. Circle the letter. Then tell if they show a direct or indirect relationship.

(a)
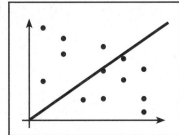

(b)
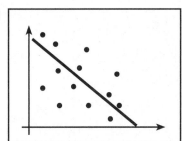

(c)
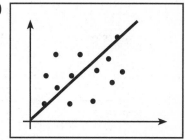

(d)
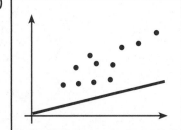

(e)
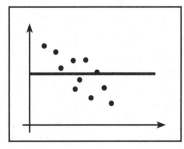

(f)
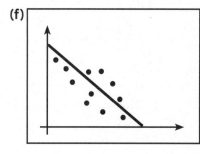

Name _____ Date _____

Activity 3

Construct a box-and-whisker plot from the set of data.

50, 73, 5, 66, 81, 100, 80, 83, 79, 88, 111, 82, 120

Activity 4

Draw a scatter plot, then tell if the plot represents a direct, indirect, or no relationship.

James took a survey of people in his class to find out if there was a relationship between how many hours people studied and how well they did on the midterm exam. He found the following results:

Name	Hours Studying	Score on Midterm
Ali	30 min	72
Laura	1 hour	75
Blake	6 hours	100
Mitch	2 hours	55
Chelsea	0 min	46
Alfred	3 hours	88
Michaela	3 hours	95
Alejo	30 min	60
Adda	5 hours	99
Jordan	5 hours	93

Name _____ Date _____

Skills Maintenance
Basic and Extended Multiplication Facts

Activity 1

Solve the basic and extended multiplication facts.

1. $4 \cdot 6 =$ _____

2. $40 \cdot 6 =$ _____

3. _____ $\cdot 3 = 24$

4. $30 \cdot$ _____ $= 240$

5. $70 \cdot 8 =$ _____

6. $7 \cdot 8 =$ _____

7. $5 \cdot$ _____ $= 20$

8. _____ $\cdot 50 = 200$

9. _____ $\cdot 9 = 630$

10. $9 \cdot$ _____ $= 63$

11. _____ $\cdot 8 = 32$

12. $80 \cdot$ _____ $= 320$

Name _____ Date _____

Apply Skills
Understanding Variables

Activity 1

Solve the multiplication facts. The missing part has been replaced with a variable. Write the answer above the variable.

1. $4 \cdot 7 = m$ 2. $x \cdot 6 = 30$ 3. $y \cdot 4 = 20$ 4. $8 \cdot s = 32$

5. $7 \cdot t = 35$ 6. $z \cdot 8 = 56$ 7. $5 \cdot 5 = k$ 8. $b \cdot 9 = 18$

Activity 2

Look at the three statements in each problem and analyze the pattern. Circle the part(s) of each statement that stay the same. Put a box around the parts that change. Replace the parts that change (the boxed numbers) with a variable and write a general statement about the pattern.

Model	$\boxed{8} \cdot \bigcirc = \bigcirc$ $\boxed{2.5} \cdot \bigcirc = \bigcirc$ $\boxed{17\frac{1}{2}} \cdot \bigcirc = \bigcirc$
	General Pattern ___ m ___ $\cdot\, 0 = 0$

1. $1 \cdot 7 = 7$

   $1 \cdot 75.8 = 75.8$

   $1 \cdot \frac{1}{4} = \frac{1}{4}$

   General Pattern _____

2. $5 + 0 = 5$

   $25 + 0 = 25$

   $\frac{1}{2} + 0 = \frac{1}{2}$

   General Pattern _____

3. $4 \div 4 = 1$

   $\frac{1}{4} \div \frac{1}{4} = 1$

   $234.9 \div 234.9 = 1$

   General Pattern _____

4. $150 - 150 = 0$

   $227.9 - 227.9 = 0$

   $\frac{3}{5} - \frac{3}{5} = 0$

   General Pattern _____

Name _____ Date _____

 Problem-Solving Activity
Strategies for Solving Problems

Tell what strategy you use to solve the problem, then solve.

1. An architect is drawing a blueprint picture of a house. She makes a square for the body of the house that is 81 square feet. There is a rectangle for the door that is 12 square feet. There is also a triangle for the roof that has a base of 9 and an area of 13.5. Find the height of the triangle.

   What is the best method of solving this problem?

   _____

2. The developers of an apartment complex in downtown Pittsburgh want people to notice their buildings from a distance. They designed the buildings to follow a pattern. There will be five apartment buildings. The first three buildings have been built. Draw rectangles to show how tall the two remaining buildings will be.

   What is the best method of solving this problem?

   _____

   Building   Building   Building   Building   Building
      A   B   C   D   E

mBook Reinforce Understanding
Use the mBook *Study Guide* to review lesson concepts.

Name _____ Date _____

Skills Maintenance
Using Variables

Activity 1

Write the missing value above the variable.

1. $m - 9 = 7$ 2. $16 \div 4 = n$

3. $8 \cdot p = 56$ 4. $r + 7 = 12$

5. $9 + 5 = t$

Activity 2

Look at the number patterns and circle the general pattern that matches.

1. $5 + 0 = 5$ $10 + 0 = 10$ $13 + 0 = 13$
    (a) $x + x = 0$
    (b) $x - x = 0$
    (c) $x + 0 = x$

2. $4 - 4 = 0$ $100 - 100 = 0$ $75 - 75 = 0$
    (a) $x + x = 0$
    (b) $x - x = 0$
    (c) $x + 0 = x$

3. $1 \cdot 5 = 5$ $1 \cdot 1 = 1$ $1 \cdot 517 = 517$
    (a) $1 \cdot x = x$
    (b) $x \cdot 1 = x$
    (c) $x \cdot x = x$

Name _____ Date _____

%÷<x Apply Skills
Patterns With More Than One Variable

Activity 1

Write a general statement using variables. Check your work by substituting values of your choice for the variables.

1. The three statements are:

   $4 + 7 + 5 = 5 + 7 + 4$

   $2 + 9 + 3 = 3 + 9 + 2$

   $1.8 + 2.5 + 3.7 = 3.7 + 2.5 + 1.8$

   Use the variables a, b, and c.

   General Statement _____

   Check your statement for $a =$ _____ , $b =$ _____ , and $c =$ _____.

   Show your work here:

2. The three statements are:

   $1 \cdot 2 \cdot 10 = 10 \cdot 2 \cdot 1$

   $5 \cdot 1 \cdot 4 = 4 \cdot 1 \cdot 5$

   $25 \cdot 2 \cdot 0 = 0 \cdot 2 \cdot 25$

   Use the variables d, e, and f.

   General Statement _____

   Check your statement for $d =$ _____ , $e =$ _____ , and $f =$ _____.

   Show your work here:

3. The three statements are:

   $0 + 75 + 25 = 0 + 25 + 75$

   $100 + 90 + 10 = 100 + 10 + 90$

   $-5 + -10 + -1 = -5 + -1 + -10$

   Use the variables x, y, and z.

   General Statement _____

   Check your statement for $x =$ _____ , $y =$ _____ , and $z =$ _____.

   Show your work here:

Name _____ Date _____

Problem-Solving Activity
More With Patterns

Look at the cards. Find the pattern in the first four cards, then draw the pattern in the fifth card. Fill in the table to help you.

Card	Triangles	Stars

What are the patterns?

_____

_____

Write the general equation for each shape using variables.

△ _____

☆ _____

mBook Reinforce Understanding
Use the mBook *Study Guide* to review lesson concepts.

Name _____ Date _____

Skills Maintenance
Basic Facts With Variables

Activity 1

Solve the basic facts. Write the answer above the variable.

1. $4 + 7 = m$

2. $x - 6 = 9$

3. $y \cdot 4 = 36$

4. $8 \div s = 2$

5. $7 \cdot t = 42$

6. $z + 8 = 17$

7. $15 - 7 = k$

8. $b \div 9 = 9$

9. $h \cdot 9 = 27$

10. $7 + 7 = v$

11. $w \cdot 8 = 32$

12. $18 - 9 = d$

Name _____ Date _____

Apply Skills
Substitution

Activity 1

Substitute the value for the variable that makes each statement true.

1. What is the value of x in $x + 12 = 17$? $x =$ _____

2. What is the value of a in $a \cdot 7 = 56$? $a =$ _____

3. What is the value of b in $45 \div 9 = b$? $b =$ _____

4. What is the value of z in $27 - z = 18$? $z =$ _____

5. What is the value of w in $39 + 47 = w$? $w =$ _____

6. What is the value of d in $d - 25 = 25$? $d =$ _____

7. What is the value of y in $5 \cdot y = 35$? $y =$ _____

Name _____ Date _____

Activity 2

Substitute values for the variables in the general statements and tell if the statements are true or false.

1. $x + y + z = y + z + x$ Substitute $x = 5$, $y = 6$ and $z = 10$.

$$x \quad + \quad y \quad + \quad z \quad = \quad y \quad + \quad z \quad + \quad x$$

$$\downarrow \qquad\quad \downarrow \qquad\quad \downarrow \qquad\quad \downarrow \qquad\quad \downarrow \qquad\quad \downarrow$$

_____ + _____ + _____ = _____ + _____ + _____

Is the statement true or false? _____

2. $x \cdot y \cdot z = z \cdot x \cdot y$ Substitute $x = 5$, $y = 6$ and $z = 10$.

$$x \quad \cdot \quad y \quad \cdot \quad z \quad = \quad z \quad \cdot \quad x \quad \cdot \quad y$$

$$\downarrow \qquad\quad \downarrow \qquad\quad \downarrow \qquad\quad \downarrow \qquad\quad \downarrow \qquad\quad \downarrow$$

_____ · _____ · _____ = _____ · _____ · _____

Is the statement true or false? _____

3. $w \cdot 0 = w$ Substitute $w = 12$.

$$w \quad \cdot \quad 0 \quad = \quad w$$

$$\downarrow \qquad\quad \downarrow \qquad\quad \downarrow$$

_____ · 0 = _____

Is the statement true or false? _____

4. $0 + d = 0$ Substitute $d = \frac{3}{4}$.

$$0 \quad + \quad d \quad = \quad 0$$

$$\downarrow \qquad\quad \downarrow$$

$$0 \quad + \quad \text{_____} \quad = \quad 0$$

Is the statement true or false? _____

5. $0 \cdot g = 0$ Substitute $g = 2.7$.

$$0 \quad \cdot \quad g \quad = \quad 0$$

$$\downarrow$$

$$0 \quad \cdot \quad \text{_____} \quad = \quad 0$$

Is the statement true or false? _____

Unit 2

Name _____ Date _____

 Problem-Solving Activity
Pattern Cards

Look at the set of pattern cards. Cards 1 and 2 have stars and triangles, but Card 3 has only triangles. Analyze the pattern in Cards 1 and 2 and tell how many stars there should be on Card 3. Then answer the questions.

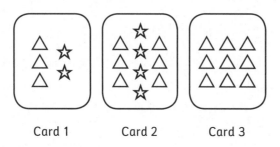

Card 1   Card 2   Card 3

1. What is the general pattern? _____

2. How many stars should go in Card 3? _____

3. How did you solve the problem?

_____

_____

_____

_____

4. Suppose you were asked to draw Card 4. Use the general pattern and substitution to demonstrate what Card 4 will look like.

mBook Reinforce Understanding
Use the mBook *Study Guide* to review lesson concepts.

Name _____ Date _____

Skills Maintenance
Using Variables

Activity 1

Substitute the correct value for the variable in each problem.

1. $x + 7 = 25$ $x =$ _____

2. $43 + b = 125$ $b =$ _____

3. $18 \div z = 3$ $z =$ _____

4. $c \div 9 = 7$ $c =$ _____

5. $400 - 300 = y$ $y =$ _____

6. $197 - a = 2$ $a =$ _____

Activity 2

Substitute the values for the variables and solve.

1. What is the value of $n + 1$ if $n = 7$? _____

2. If $2 + x = 8$, what is the value of x? _____

3. What is the value of $4 + y$ if $y = 18$? _____

4. Solve $n - 8$ if $n = 17$. _____

5. If $z = 25$, solve $z \div 5$. _____

6. What is the value of $m \div 9$ if $m = 81$? _____

Unit 2

Name _____ Date _____

%÷ Apply Skills
Ratios

Activity 1

Use three methods for writing ratios based on the hand of five cards.

1. What is the ratio of hearts to diamonds?

   _____ hearts to _____ diamonds

   _____   _____

2. What is the ratio of spades to the entire hand?

   _____ spades to _____ entire hand

   _____   _____

3. What is the ratio of 3s to the entire hand?

   _____ 3s to _____ entire hand

   _____   _____

4. What is the ratio of 3s to 7s in this hand?

   _____ 3s to _____ 7s

   _____   _____

5. What is the ratio of clubs to the entire hand?

   _____ clubs to _____ entire hand

   _____   _____

6. Explain why it's important to label the things you are comparing in the ratios.

   _____

   _____

   _____

Name _____ Date _____

Problem-Solving Activity
Word Problems With Ratios

Now it is your turn to solve some ratio word problems. Remember to start with the labels. This will tell you what numbers to look for in the problem. If the numbers are not there, you will need to compute them. Then connect the labels with the numbers and write the answer as a ratio.

1. Your math class has 27 students. There are 12 seniors and the rest are juniors. What is the senior-to-junior ratio?

   _____

2. The football team has 12 wins and 6 losses. What is the win-to-loss ratio?

   _____

3. There are 3 bird owners, 4 cat owners, and 2 dog owners in a complex of 18 apartments. All other owners have no pets. What is the bird-owner to cat-owner ratio?

   _____

4. If there are 300 students in the sophomore class and 180 of them are girls, what is the boy-to-girl ratio?

   _____

5. If the recipe calls for 1 cup sugar and 2 eggs, what is the sugar-to-egg ratio?

   _____

6. Suppose you are dealt 5 hearts, 3 diamonds, 1 spade, and 1 club. What is the ratio of hearts to the entire hand of cards?

   _____

mBook Reinforce Understanding
Use the mBook *Study Guide* to review lesson concepts.

Unit 2

Name _____ Date _____

 Skills Maintenance
Variables and Substitution

Activity 1

Substitute the given value for the variable and solve.

1. $x + 50$
   Substitute $x = 25$.
   Solve _____

2. $y - 112$
   Substitute $y = 500$.
   Solve _____

3. $30 \cdot w$
   Substitute $w = 50$.
   Solve _____

4. $m \div 20$
   Substitute $m = 100$.
   Solve _____

5. $500 - n$
   Substitute $n = 250$
   Solve _____

Activity 2

Tell the ratio in each of the problems.

1. There are 25 dogs at the kennel and 15 cats. What is the dog-to-cat ratio?

   _____

2. There are 12 girls in a classroom of 22 students. What is the girl-to-boy ratio?

   _____

3. A recipe calls for 3 cups of sugar and 1 cup of flour. What is the flour-to-sugar ratio in the recipe?

   _____

Name _____ Date _____

 Apply Skills
Using Variables in Formulas

> **Activity 1**

Use the squares on the grid to help you measure the shapes. Find the area of each shape using the appropriate formula. Label your answer in square units.

Area of a rectangle = $l \cdot w$
Area of a triangle = $\frac{1}{2} \cdot b \cdot h$
Area of a circle = $3.14 \cdot r^2$

1. $r = $ _____

   Area of circle _____

2. $b = $ _____

   $h = $ _____

   Area of triangle _____

3. $l = $ _____

   $w = $ _____

   Area of rectangle _____

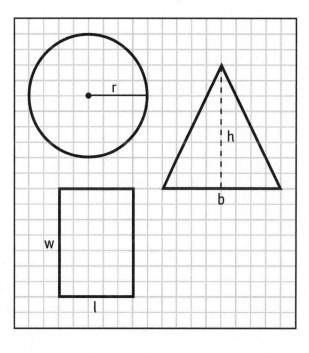

Name _____ Date _____

Activity 2

Substitute the values for the variables in each of the formulas and solve for the missing part.

1. The area of the triangle is 10 square units.

   What is the base? _____

   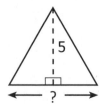

   Area Formula for a Triangle:

   $A = \frac{1}{2} \cdot b \cdot h$

2. The area of the parallelogram is 30 square units.

   What is the height? _____

   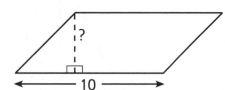

   Area Formula for a Parallelogram:

   $A = b \cdot h$

3. The area of the triangle is 8 square units.

   What is the height? _____

   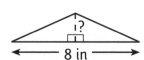

   Area Formula for a Triangle:

   $A = \frac{1}{2} \cdot b \cdot h$

4. The area of the rectangle is 27 square units.

   What is the base? _____

   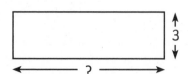

   Area Formula for a Rectangle:

   $A = b \cdot h$

mBook **Reinforce Understanding**
Use the mBook *Study Guide* to review lesson concepts.

Name _____ Date _____

Skills Maintenance
Variables and Substitution

Activity 1

Substitute a value for the variable that makes the statement true.

1. $30 \cdot w = 90$ $w =$ _____

2. $120 - z = 40$ $z =$ _____

3. $m + 30 = 50$ $m =$ _____

4. $80 \div 4 = x$ $x =$ _____

5. $y = 12.7 - 2.5$ $y =$ _____

6. $12.5 \cdot u = 12.5$ $u =$ _____

Activity 2

Substitute the values for the variables in the formulas and solve.

1. Area of a triangle $= \frac{1}{2} \cdot b \cdot h$

   What is the area of a triangle with a base of 5 and a height of 6?

   _____

2. Area of a parallelogram $= b \cdot h$

   What is the base of a parallelogram with an area of 48 and a height of 6?

   _____

3. Circumference of a circle $= 2 \cdot \pi \cdot r$. (Remember, we round pi to 3.14.)

   What is the circumference of a circle with a radius of 2?

   _____

Unit 2

Name _____ Date _____

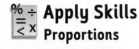 **Apply Skills**
Proportions

Activity 1

Look at the proportions with missing parts. Analyze the numbers to find
the multiplication pattern. Then find the value of the variable.

1. $\frac{4}{5} = \frac{x}{20}$ $x =$ _____

2. $\frac{1}{4} = \frac{4}{y}$ $y =$ _____

3. $\frac{w}{9} = \frac{3}{27}$ $w =$ _____

4. $\frac{2}{3} = \frac{14}{z}$ $z =$ _____

Activity 2

Select the two cards that are proportional, then write the proportion.

1. Which two cards are proportional?
(Circle the two cards)

Write the proportion: _____ = _____

Card 1   Card 2   Card 3

2. Which two cards are proportional?
(Circle the two cards)

Write the proportion: _____ = _____

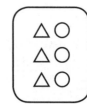 

Card 1   Card 2   Card 3

3. Which two cards are proportional?
(Circle the two cards)

Write the proportion: _____ = _____

Card 1   Card 2   Card 3

Name _____ Date _____

Problem-Solving Activity
Solving Word Problems Using Proportions

Solve the problems by setting up a proportion.

1. Blake is painting his house a shade of green. The paint is 2 parts green paint to 1 part white paint. How much white paint will he need to add to 12 cans of green paint?

    _____

2. Tyrone needs to increase the recipe on the back of the pancake box. The recipe calls for 1 cup mix and 2 cups water. If he uses 8 cups of mix, how much water will he need?

    _____

3. Elyse and Sam are building a bridge for their physics class. They need 2 bottles of craft glue for every 60 wood sticks they put together. They have a box of 360 wood sticks. How many bottles of glue will they need?

    _____

4. When you dye eggs, you need 2 tablespoons of vinegar and 3 cups of water for each color tablet. Suppose you are mixing the dye for 6 different color tablets. How much vinegar will you need? How much water?

    _____

mBook **Reinforce Understanding**
Use the mBook *Study Guide* to review lesson concepts.

Name _____ Date _____

Skills Maintenance
Using Variables

Activity 1

Substitute a value for the variable and solve.

1. What is $x + 198$ if $x = 107$? _____

2. What is $40 \cdot y$ if $y = 8$? _____

3. What is $63 \div w$ if $w = 9$? _____

4. What is $807 - z$ if $z = 299$? _____

Activity 2

Tell the area of each by substituting values for the variables.

1. $A = \frac{1}{2} \cdot b \cdot h$

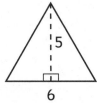

What is the area?

_____

2. $A = b \cdot h$

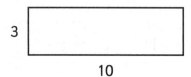

What is the area?

_____

3. $A = b \cdot h$

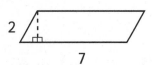

What is the area?

_____

4. $A = s^2$

What is the area?

_____

Name _____ Date _____

Apply Skills
Translating Word Statements Into Number Statements

Activity 1

Write variables for each of the word statements. Then write a number statement.

1. Sam is 3 years older than his brother Terrell. Write a number statement about Sam's age.

    The variable _____ stands for _____ and the variable _____ stands for _____ .

    Number statement _____

2. In the middle of the summer, the sun sets about 3 hours later than it does in the middle of the winter. Write a number statement that describes the time the sun sets.

    The variable _____ stands for _____ and the variable _____ stands for _____ .

    Number statement _____

3. Two men are rock climbing. The first man always stays 10 feet higher than the other man as they climb the rock. Write a number statement about how high up the first man is.

    The variable _____ stands for _____ and the variable _____ stands for _____

    Number statement _____

4. There are four times as many students as adults on the field trip. Write a number statement about the number of adults on the field trip.

    The variable _____ stands for _____ and the variable _____ stands for _____ .

    Number statement _____

    If there are 8 adults on the field trip, how many students are there?

    Number Statement _____

Name _____ Date _____

 ## Problem-Solving Activity
More Proportions With Variables

Draw pattern cards based on a proportion with a missing part. First solve
the proportion by finding the value of the variable in the proportion. Then
draw the pattern cards that reflect the proportional relationship.

1. ♡ ◯ $\frac{2}{3} = \frac{x}{6}$ x = _____

2. ☺ ☐ $\frac{3}{4} = \frac{9}{w}$ w = _____

3. △ ☆ $\frac{1}{8} = \frac{2}{u}$ u = _____

	Card A	Card B
Problem 1:		
Problem 2:		
Problem 3:		

Name _____ Date _____

Problem-Solving Activity
More Proportions With Variables

Two of the five cards are proportional. Which ones are they? Once you have identified them, write the proportion and explain how you found them.

_____

_____

_____

_____

mBook Reinforce Understanding
Use the mBook *Study Guide* to review lesson concepts.

Name _____ Date _____

 Skills Maintenance
Basic Facts With Variables and Word Problems

Activity 1

Solve the problems involving variables.

1. $x + 8 = 17$ $x =$ _____

2. $y - 7 = 9$ $y =$ _____

3. $a \cdot 9 = 72$ $a =$ _____

4. $56 \div 8 = b$ $b =$ _____

5. $6 + c = 13$ $c =$ _____

6. $14 - d = 7$ $d =$ _____

Activity 2

Select the number statement that translates the word statement.

1. Amy is 5 years older than Bob. If m represents Amy's age and x represents Bob's age:

   (a) $m = 5 \cdot x$

   (b) $x - 5 = m$

   (c) $m - 5 = x$

2. There are 5 times as many students as teachers at the junior high school. If z represents the number of students and b represents the number of teachers:

   (a) $5 + z = b$

   (b) $5 \cdot b = z$

   (c) $z \cdot 5 = b$

3. There are 3 more dogs than cats at the kennel. If d represents the number of dogs and c represents the number of cats:

   (a) $3 + c = d$

   (b) $3 + d = c$

   (c) $d \cdot 3 = c$

Name _____ Date _____

 Apply Skills
Translating Number Statements Into Word Statements

Activity 1

Then write a word sentence that represents each number sentence.

1. $a + b = 12$

   If a represents _____ and b represents

   _____:

   Word Statement _____

   _____

   _____

   _____

   _____

2. $4 \cdot c = d$

   If c represents _____ and d represents

   _____:

   Word Statement _____

   _____

   _____

   _____

3. $f - 5 = m$

   If f represents _____ and m represents

   _____:

   Word Statement _____

   _____

   _____

   _____

   _____

Name _____ Date _____

Problem-Solving Activity
Identifying Proportions

Decide which cards are proportional to each other. The cards may be used more than once.

A   B   C   D

E   F   G   H

Which cards are proportional?

_____

_____

_____

_____

_____

What is the card that is not proportional to any of the others?

_____

Name _____ Date _____

Skills Maintenance
Writing Proportions

Activity 1

Find the value of the variable in the proportions.

1. $\frac{4}{6} = \frac{x}{3}$ $x =$ _____

2. $\frac{2}{3} = \frac{10}{y}$ $y =$ _____

3. $\frac{1}{a} = \frac{5}{30}$ $a =$ _____

4. $\frac{w}{3} = \frac{6}{9}$ $w =$ _____

5. $\frac{3}{4} = \frac{6}{z}$ $z =$ _____

6. $\frac{3}{m} = \frac{15}{35}$ $m =$ _____

Unit 2

Name _____ Date _____

Problem-Solving Activity
Proportions and Geometry

Circle the two similar shapes in each set of three shapes.

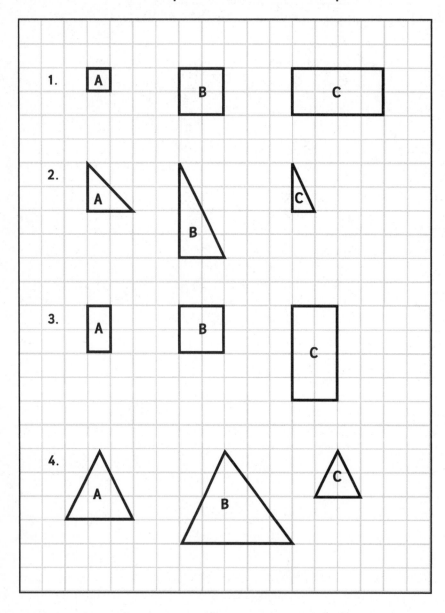

Name _____ Date _____

Problem-Solving Activity
Proportions and Geometry

Find the dimensions of the shapes. Write proportions that prove each pair of shapes is similar. Then tell what the scaling factor is.

Problem 1

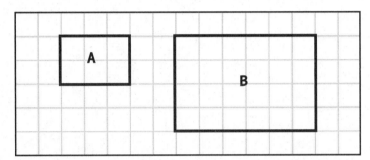

The dimensions of A are → base _____ height _____

The dimensions of B are → base _____ height _____

Write a proportion about the dimensions of the two shapes that proves they are similar.

A   B

$\dfrac{\text{Base}}{\text{Height}}$ _____ = _____ What is the scaling factor? _____

Problem 2

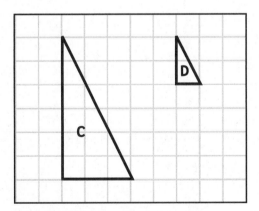

The dimensions of C are → base _____ height _____

The dimensions of D are → base _____ height _____

Write a proportion about the dimensions of the two shapes that proves they are similar.

C   D

$\dfrac{\text{Base}}{\text{Height}}$ _____ = _____ What is the scaling factor? _____

Name _____ Date _____

Problem-Solving Activity
Using Proportions in Geometry

Now it is your turn to make similar shapes. Use the grid paper and draw the first shape, A. Draw a second shape, B, which is similar to A. Write the proportion. What is the scaling factor? Draw another shape, C, that is proportional to A. Write the proportion. What is the scaling factor you used for this shape?

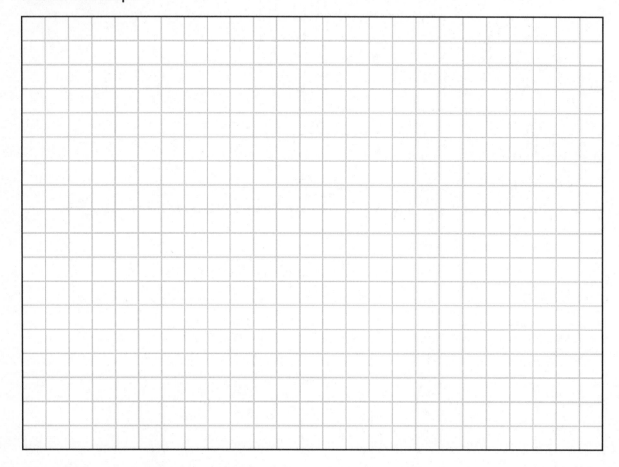

1. Write the proportion showing that Shapes A and B are similar.

   Shape A   Shape B

   $\dfrac{\text{Base}}{\text{Height}}$ _____ = _____ What scaling factor did you use? _____

2. Write the proportion showing that Shapes A and C are similar.

   Shape A   Shape C

   $\dfrac{\text{Base}}{\text{Height}}$ _____ = _____ What scaling factor did you use? _____

Name _____ Date _____

Skills Maintenance
Translations and Proportions

Activity 1

Select the best translation for each statement.

1. Jessica is 4 inches taller than Bonnie. If j is Jessica's height and b is Bonnie's height:

    (a) $j = b + 4$

    (b) $b = j + 4$

    (c) $b - 4 = j$

2. $W - 4 = L$

    If W is Wanda's age and L is Lenny's age:

    (a) Wanda is 4 years younger than Lenny.

    (b) Lenny is 4 years younger than Wanda.

    (c) Lenny and Wanda are the same age.

Activity 2

Write a proportion about the dimensions of the similar shapes. Tell what the scaling factor is.

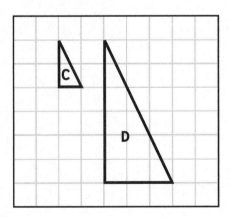

Proportion _____

Scaling factor _____

Name _____ Date _____

 ## Problem-Solving Activity
Figuring Out the Formula

Find the formula for each set of input and output data given.

1.

Input	Output
45	9
30	6
60	12
50	10
20	4

What is the formula for this data? Use N for input and M for output. Formula _____

2.

Input	Output
6	48
12	96
4	32
5	40
1	8

What is the formula for this data? Use x for input and y for output. Formula _____

3.

Input	Output
20	25
35	40
75	80
10	15

What is the formula for this data? Use w for input and z for output. Formula _____

Name _____ Date _____

 Problem-Solving Activity
Figuring Out the Formula

Fill in the missing input, output, or formula for each of the problems.

1.

Input	Formula	Output
$n = 6$		
$n = 8$	$n \cdot 8 = w$	
$n = 10$		
$n = 1.5$		

2.

Input	Formula	Output
$n = 6$		$w = 3$
$n = 8$		$w = 4$
$n = 10$		$w = 5$
$n = 12$		$w = 6$

3.

Input	Formula	Output
		$w = 20$
	$n + 10 = w$	$w = 13$
		$w = 27$
		$w = 109$

mBook **Reinforce Understanding**
Use the mBook *Study Guide* to review lesson concepts.

Name _____ Date _____

 Skills Maintenance
Proportions

Activity 1

Write the value for the variable.

1. $\dfrac{a}{16} = \dfrac{1}{4}$ $a =$ _____

2. $\dfrac{b}{24} = \dfrac{1}{6}$ $b =$ _____

3. $\dfrac{2}{3} = \dfrac{c}{15}$ $c =$ _____

4. $\dfrac{3}{4} = \dfrac{9}{d}$ $d =$ _____

5. $\dfrac{1}{e} = \dfrac{5}{30}$ $e =$ _____

6. $\dfrac{1}{2} = \dfrac{20}{f}$ $f =$ _____

Name _____ Date _____

 ## Problem-Solving Activity
Proportions and Map Reading

Set up a proportion to compute the actual distance in miles between cities on a map. Use the scale 1 inch = 50 miles.

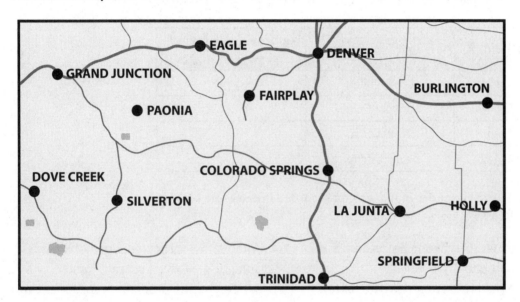

1. Dove Creek and La Junta are 4 inches apart on the map. Write a proportion with a variable to compute the distance in miles.

    $\dfrac{\text{Inches}}{\text{Miles}}$ _____ = _____

    Write the proportion again, replacing the variable with its value.

    $\dfrac{\text{Inches}}{\text{Miles}}$ _____ = _____

    What is the distance between Dove Creek and La Junta in miles? _____ miles

2. Dove Creek and Holly are 5 inches apart on the map. Write a proportion with a variable to compute the distance in miles.

    $\dfrac{\text{Inches}}{\text{Miles}}$ _____ = _____

    Write the proportion again, replacing the variable with its value.

    $\dfrac{\text{Inches}}{\text{Miles}}$ _____ = _____

    What is the distance between Dove Creek and Holly in miles? _____ miles

Name _____ Date _____

Problem-Solving Activity
Proportions and Map Reading

Turn to the map on page 199 of the *Student Textbook*. The scale for this map is 1 inch = 5 miles. Use your thumb as an informal measuring tool, and record the distances to the nearest inch.

Starting Point	Ending Point	Approximate Inches Between Points
Lookout Point	Crow Valley	
Canyon View	Lookout Point	
Devils Kitchen	Crow Valley	
Ute Canyon View	Devils Kitchen	

Use the approximate distances in inches you recorded in the table to answer the questions.

1. What is the actual mileage between Lookout Point and Crow Valley?
   a. Set up the proportion statement with a variable.

   $\dfrac{\text{Inches}}{\text{Miles}} =$

   b. Find the value of the variable.

   $\dfrac{\text{Inches}}{\text{Miles}} =$

   Answer _____

2. What is the actual mileage between Canyon View and Lookout Point?
   a. Set up the proportion statement with a variable.

   $\dfrac{\text{Inches}}{\text{Miles}} =$

   b. Find the value of the variable.

   $\dfrac{\text{Inches}}{\text{Miles}} =$

   Answer _____

3. What is the actual mileage between the Devils Kitchen and Crow Valley?
   a. Set up the proportion statement with a variable.

   $\dfrac{\text{Inches}}{\text{Miles}} =$

   b. Find the value of the variable.

   $\dfrac{\text{Inches}}{\text{Miles}} =$

   Answer _____

4. What is the actual mileage between Ute Canyon View and Devils Kitchen?
   a. Set up the proportion statement with a variable.

   $\dfrac{\text{Inches}}{\text{Miles}} =$

   b. Find the value of the variable.

   $\dfrac{\text{Inches}}{\text{Miles}} =$

   Answer _____

mBook Reinforce Understanding
Use the mBook *Study Guide* to review lesson concepts.

Name _____ Date _____

Skills Maintenance
Variables and Proportions

Activity 1

Convert the percents to decimal numbers.

1. 75% _____

2. 4% _____

3. 16% _____

4. 55% _____

5. 2% _____

6. 85% _____

Activity 2

For each group of shapes, select the two that are similar.

1. Which shapes are similar?

   (a) A and B

   (b) A and C

   (c) B and C

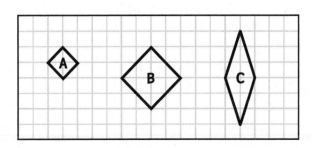

2. Which shapes are similar?

   (a) A and B

   (b) A and C

   (c) B and C

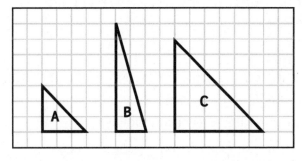

3. Which shapes are similar?

   (a) A and B

   (b) A and C

   (c) B and C

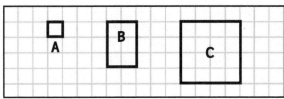

Name _____ Date _____

Problem-Solving Activity
Translating Percent Problems

Solve the percent problems by substituting the value for the variables. You may use a calculator.

1. What is the discount on a $500 TV that is 15% off?   Answer _____
    D = discount, p = percent off, c = cost

    $$D \quad = \quad p \quad \cdot \quad c$$
    $$\downarrow \qquad \downarrow \qquad \downarrow$$
    _____ = _____ $\cdot$ _____

2. What is the tax on a $300 item at a tax rate of 7%?   Answer _____
    T = tax amount, r = tax rate, c = cost

    $$T \quad = \quad r \quad \cdot \quad c$$
    $$\downarrow \qquad \downarrow \qquad \downarrow$$
    _____ = _____ $\cdot$ _____

3. What is a 15% tip on a $100 meal at a restaurant?   Answer _____
    T = tip, r = percent, c = cost of meal

    $$T \quad = \quad r \quad \cdot \quad c$$
    $$\downarrow \qquad \downarrow \qquad \downarrow$$
    _____ = _____ $\cdot$ _____

4. How much interest will you earn on $1,500 at 2%?   Answer _____
    I = interest, r = rate, a = account balance

    $$T \quad = \quad r \quad \cdot \quad c$$
    $$\downarrow \qquad \downarrow \qquad \downarrow$$
    _____ = _____ $\cdot$ _____

5. What is the discount on a $250 item at 20% off?   Answer _____
    D = discount, p = percent off, c = cost

    $$D \quad = \quad p \quad \cdot \quad c$$
    $$\downarrow \qquad \downarrow \qquad \downarrow$$
    _____ = _____ $\cdot$ _____

6. How much tax will you pay for a $75 item at a 6% rate.   Answer _____
    T = tax, r = tax rate, c = cost

    $$T \quad = \quad r \quad \cdot \quad c$$
    $$\downarrow \qquad \downarrow \qquad \downarrow$$
    _____ = _____ $\cdot$ _____

Name _____ Date _____

Problem-Solving Activity
Translating Percent Problems

Solve the percent problems. Remember to convert the percent to a decimal number before you multiply. You may use a calculator.

1. Everything in a department store is on sale for 10% off. Write an equation to describe the discount on a $500 digital camera.

   _____

2. Roseanne has a coupon for 5% off her monthly phone bill. Write an equation to describe the discount on her $175 bill.

   _____

3. The teacher promised the class bonus points for the semester. She would give each student a bonus of 10% of the total homework points for the semester. Write an equation that describes how many bonus points Bonnie will get if she earned 150 homework points during the semester.

   _____

4. The New Jax Band is donating 1% of all ticket sales from a concert tour to charity. Write an equation that describes how much they will donate to the charity if they sell $1,500 in tickets.

   _____

mBook **Reinforce Understanding**
Use the mBook *Study Guide* to review lesson concepts.

Name _____ Date _____

 Skills Maintenance
Variables and Proportions

Activity 1

Solve the percent problems by filling in the values of the variables.

1. Micah found a great sale on his favorite soccer cleats. They are 75% off. If the original cost is $150, what is the discount? _____

2. Sheila bought $140 worth of clothing at a store in a state where the sales tax is 6%. How much tax will she pay on her purchase? _____

3. If you tip 15%, how much is the tip for a meal that costs $58.89? _____

4. Adrianne has been saving money in an account since her 1st birthday. On her 16th birthday, she realized she had $2,500 in the account. If the interest rate is 5%, how much interest will she earn this year? _____

Name _____ Date _____

 **Apply Skills**
Simplifying Ratios

Activity 1

Tell if the ratio can be simplified. Circle Y for yes or N for no.

1. Ratio of boys to girls is 12:13.   Y   or   N

2. $\dfrac{\text{Dogs}}{\text{Cats}} = \dfrac{2}{4}$ Y   or   N

3. Ratio of hearts to diamonds is 6:9.   Y   or   N

4. $\dfrac{\text{Milk}}{\text{Mix}}$ $\dfrac{4 \text{ cups}}{5 \text{ cups}}$ Y   or   N

5. Ratio of circle to squares is 8:12.   Y   or   N

6. Ratio of stars to moons is 2:3.   Y   or   N

Name _____ Date _____

Activity 2

Simplify each ratio. List the common factors, then tell what the GCF is.
Write the equation that shows the original ratio, simplified fraction, and
whole number you divided by.

1. $\dfrac{\text{Completed Passes}}{\text{Interceptions}}$ $\dfrac{12}{8}$

   Factors of 12 _____

   Factors of 8 _____

   Greatest common factor _____

   $\dfrac{12}{8} =$

   Simplified ratio _____

2. $\dfrac{\text{Hours}}{\text{Miles}}$ $\dfrac{4}{16}$

   Factors of 4 _____

   Factors of 16 _____

   Greatest common factor _____

   $\dfrac{4}{16} =$

   Simplified ratio _____

3. $\dfrac{\text{boys}}{\text{girls}}$ $\dfrac{12}{14}$

   Factors of 12 _____

   Factors of 14 _____

   Greatest common factor _____

   $\dfrac{12}{14} =$

   Simplified ratio _____

4. $\dfrac{\text{Inches}}{\text{Miles}}$ $\dfrac{5}{25}$

   Factors of 5 _____

   Factors of 25 _____

   Greatest common factor _____

   $\dfrac{5}{25} =$

   Simplified ratio _____

Name _____ Date _____

Problem-Solving Activity
Complex Pattern Cards

Find the proportional relationships in the pattern cards. Remember, the multiplication patterns may not be obvious. You may have to reduce the ratios in order to find the proportional relationships. Four of the six pattern cards are proportional. Circle the proportional cards.

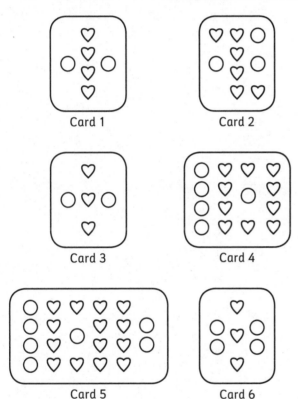

Card 1

Card 2

Card 3

Card 4

Card 5

Card 6

What is the reduced ratio that helped you find the proportional cards? _____

mBook Reinforce Understanding
Use the mBook *Study Guide* to review lesson concepts.

Name _____ Date _____

Skills Maintenance
Translating Percent Problems

Activity 1

Solve the percent problems.

1. The tax rate is 6% and your purchase is $250. How much tax will you pay?

   _____ • _____ = _____

2. What is the 15% tip for a $80 meal?

   _____ • _____ = _____

3. What is the interest earned on $3,000 at a 3% rate?

   _____ • _____ = _____

4. What is the discount amount for 25% off from $50?

   _____ • _____ = _____

Name _____ Date _____

Apply Skills
Making Sense of Proportional Reasoning

Activity 1

Color each set of spinners so there is an equal chance of landing on a colored section in both spinners.

1.

Drawing 1   **Drawing 2**

2.

Drawing 1   **Drawing 2**

3.

Drawing 1   **Drawing 2**

4.

 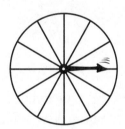

Drawing 1   **Drawing 2**

Name _____ Date _____

Activity 2

Answer the questions about proportions.

1. The two jars of marbles have dark and light marbles in them. Each jar has a different amount of marbles. Are the chances of drawing a dark marble from each jar the same or different? If they are different, which drawing gives you the best chance of drawing a dark marble?

   _____

   _____

   _____

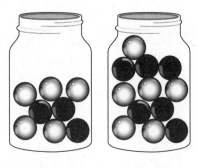

   Drawing 1   **Drawing 2**

2. You can make chocolate milk from chocolate syrup and milk. The syrup is what makes it taste sweet. Does each glass of chocolate milk taste the same or is one glass sweeter than the other?

   _____

   _____

   3 ounces of syrup   **5 ounces of syrup**
   6 ounces of milk   **10 ounces of milk**

mBook Reinforce Understanding
Use the mBook *Study Guide* to review lesson concepts.

Name _____ Date _____

 ## Skills Maintenance
Word Statements With Variables

Activity 1

Select the word statement that is the best translation of the number statement.

1. $a + 5 = c$

   If a is Allen's age and c is Colleen's age:

   (a) Allen is 5 years older than Colleen.

   (b) Colleen is 5 years older than Allen.

   (c) Allen is 5 times as old as Colleen.

2. $w \cdot 10 = x$

   If w is the number of dogs and x is the number of fish:

   (a) There are 10 times as many dogs as fish at the pet store.

   (b) There are 10 fewer fish than dogs at the pet store.

   (c) There are 10 times as many fish as dogs at the pet store.

3. $x - 4 = y$

   If x is the number of cookies and y is the number of brownies:

   (a) There are 4 fewer cookies than brownies.

   (b) There are 4 more cookies than brownies.

   (c) There are 4 fewer brownies than cookies.

Name _____ Date _____

Unit Review
Variables

Activity 1

Find the areas of the rectangles. Remember the formula: Area = *l* • *w*.
Label your answer in square units.

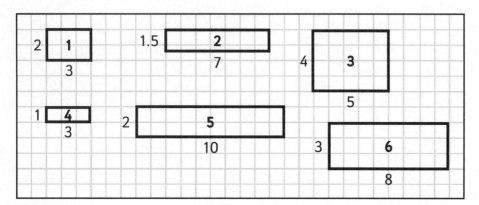

1. Area _____

2. Area _____

3. Area _____

4. Area _____

5. Area _____

6. Area _____

Activity 2

Find the value of the missing variable in the proportions.

1. $\frac{1}{4} = \frac{y}{20}$ $y =$ _____

2. $\frac{3}{m} = \frac{6}{4}$ $m =$ _____

3. $\frac{t}{18} = \frac{1}{2}$ $t =$ _____

4. $\frac{7}{10} = \frac{x}{50}$ $x =$ _____

5. $\frac{11}{h} = \frac{22}{4}$ $h =$ _____

6. $\frac{r}{6} = \frac{36}{36}$ $r =$ _____

Name _____ Date _____

Activity 3

Translate the word statements to number statements, and the number statements to word statements. Solve if necessary.

1. $m = j + 6$

   $m =$ _____

   $j =$ _____

   Statement _____

   _____

2. A store is going out of business and everything is 80% off. If a TV was originally $635, how much is it after the discount?

   _____

3. You go out to a restaurant and decide to tip your waitress 20% on a $53 bill. How much is the tip?

   _____

4. A teacher notices that a student is absent twice as much as you are. Write an equation using variables.

   _____

Unit 2

Name _____ Date _____

Unit Review
Ratios and Proportions

Activity 1

Write a ratio for each word statement. Then say if the ratio is a part-to-part or part-to-whole relationship.

1. 10 computers to 3 printers

    Ratio _____   Relationship _____

2. 1 pepper out of a barrel of 12

    Ratio _____   Relationship _____

3. 3 missed calls out of 14

    Ratio _____   Relationship _____

4. 4 pizzas to 1 cake

    Ratio _____   Relationship _____

Activity 2

Circle the cards that are proportional to each other.

Card 1   Card 2   Card 3   Card 4   Card 5

Name _____ Date _____

Activity 3

Find the ratios of the shapes in the grid to decide if they are proportional or not. Circle the shapes that are proportional.

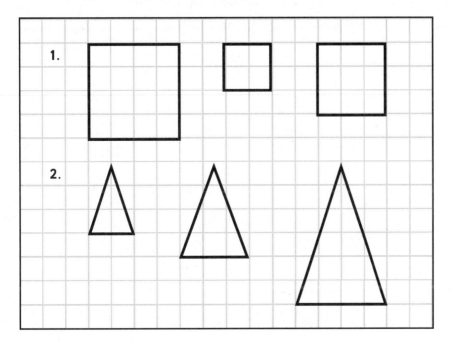

1. _____

2. _____

Name _____ Date _____

Skills Maintenance
Using Variables

Activity 1

Find the value of the variable in each equation. Write the answer above the variable.

1. $6 \cdot 80 = \underline{\quad y \quad}$

2. $7 \cdot 8 = \underline{\quad m \quad}$

3. $40 \div \underline{\quad n \quad} = 20$

4. $\underline{\quad s \quad} - 4 = 55$

5. $5 \cdot 11 = \underline{\quad z \quad}$

6. $70 - 30 = \underline{\quad w \quad}$

7. $\underline{\quad b \quad} + 20 = 32$

8. $6 \cdot 9 = \underline{\quad a \quad}$

9. $30 \div 10 = \underline{\quad g \quad}$

Name _____ Date _____

Apply Skills
Inequalities

Activity 1

Use words to describe what the symbols mean in the inequalities.

Model	The inequality $x > 5$ means x is <u>greater than 5</u> .

1. The inequality $x < 4$ means x is _____ .

2. The inequality $y \leq 3$ means y is _____ .

3. The inequality $5 \geq z$ means 5 is _____ .

4. The inequality $6 > w$ means 6 is _____ .

5. The inequality $m < 14$ means m is _____ .

6. The inequality $s \geq 200$ means s is _____ .

Name _____ Date _____

Activity 2

Draw each of the inequalities on the number lines provided. Remember to use an open circle when you use the symbols > or <, and to fill in the circle when you use the symbols ≥ or ≤.

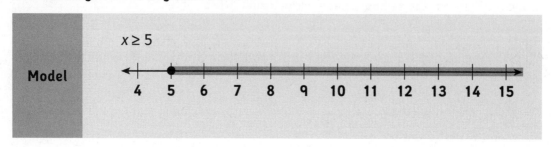

Model $x \geq 5$

1. $y > 7$

2. $z \geq 10$

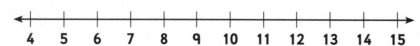

3. $8 > y$

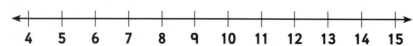

4. $y \geq 7$

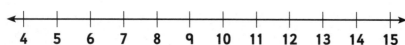

5. $m \leq 31$

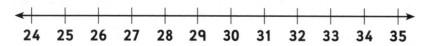

Name _____ Date _____

Problem-Solving Activity
Rate

Find the rate for each problem by answering these questions:
What is the comparison? What is the rate proportion?

1. Williams Building Company builds new houses in the Cincinnati
    area. They just finished a project that involved 45 new homes. Part
    of their work involves painting the inside of the house. A gallon of
    paint costs $10. It takes 2 gallons of paint for 100 square feet of
    wall space. The inside of the normal house needs 400 square feet to
    be painted. How much will the paint cost for one house?

    _____

    _____

2. A fire hose can be used to spray water on a large area. The hose
    can spray 100 gallons of water in 4 minutes. It can take over 2
    hours to put out a fire in a small house. How many gallons of water
    will firefighters use in 20 minutes?

    _____

    _____

3. Shandra is the starting guard on the Wildcats basketball team.
    She is almost 6 feet tall, and she has scored 60 points in the first
    3 games. How many points do you expect her to score in 15 games?

    _____

    _____

4. Carlo works at a factory that makes potato chips. He works six
    hours a day loading boxes onto trucks. The factory can produce
    1 box filled with bags of potato chips every 4 minutes. How many
    boxes filled with chips does the factory make in 20 minutes?

    _____

    _____

mBook Reinforce Understanding
Use the mBook *Study Guide* to review lesson concepts.

Name _____ Date _____

Skills Maintenance
Inequalities

Activity 1

Show the range of values on the number line that make the inequality true.

1. $x \leq 0$

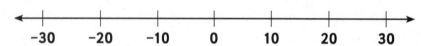

-30   -20   -10   0   10   20   30

2. $b < 293$

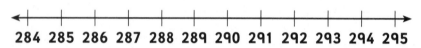

284 285 286 287 288 289 290 291 292 293 294 295

3. $a \geq -10$

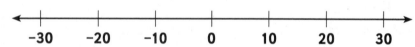

-30   -20   -10   0   10   20   30

4. $a \geq 39$

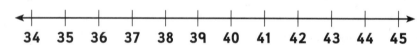

34   35   36   37   38   39   40   41   42   43   44   45

5. $c > -5$

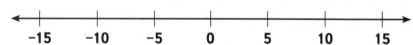

-15   -10   -5   0   5   10   15

Name _____ Date _____

%÷ Apply Skills
=< ×
Translating Inequalities Using > and <

> **Activity 1**

Read each word problem. Choose a variable for the inequality. Write the inequality, then graph it on a number line.

Model

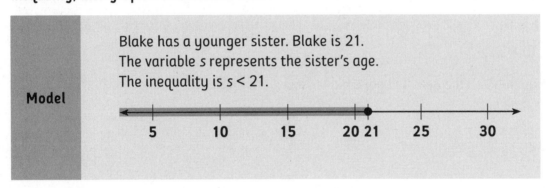

Blake has a younger sister. Blake is 21.
The variable *s* represents the sister's age.
The inequality is *s* < 21.

1. Todd has an older sister who is 16.

   The variable _____ represents _____ .

   The inequality is _____ .

   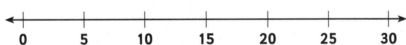

2. Bev is in a higher grade at school than Billy. Billy is in the third grade.

   The variable _____ represents _____ .

   The inequality is _____ .

3. Bob is taller than Bud. Bud is 6 feet tall.

   The variable _____ represents _____ .

   The inequality is _____ .

4. Kyle has more CDs than his sister. His sister has 10 CDs.

   The variable _____ represents _____ .

   The inequality is _____ .

   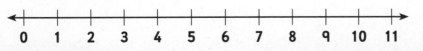

Name _____ Date _____

Activity 2

Select the best inequality for each word statement.

1. Becca scored more points than Patty. Patty scored 10 points.
   If b = Becca's score:

   (a) $b > 10$

   (b) $b < 10$

   (c) $10 > b$

2. Tom got a 95 on the quiz. Ted got a higher score than Tom.
   If x = Ted's score:

   (a) $95 > x$

   (b) $x < 95$

   (c) $x > 95$

3. Lynda is older than Suzy. Lynda is 15.
   If y is Suzy's age:

   (a) $y > 15$

   (b) $y < 15$

   (c) $15 < y$

4. The temperature rose above 40.
   If t is the temperature:

   (a) $t > 40$

   (b) $40 > t$

   (c) $t < 40$

Name _____ Date _____

Problem-Solving Activity
Decreasing and Increasing Rates

Read each word problem. Then write a rate proportion with a variable to solve the problem. Remember to think about what you are multiplying by when you solve the problem.

1. If Bobbi can run 4 miles in an hour, how long does it take her to run 1 mile?

    _____

2. Elizabeth likes to read. She prides herself on being able to read 240 pages in 2 hours. How long does it take Elizabeth to read 60 pages?

    _____

3. The captain of the soccer team scored 24 goals in 6 games. At this rate, how many goals does he score per game?

    _____

4. If it takes you 6 hours to drive 360 miles, how many miles can you drive in an hour?

    _____

mBook Reinforce Understanding
Use the mBook *Study Guide* to review lesson concepts.

Unit 3 • Lesson 2   **103**

Name _____ Date _____

Skills Maintenance
Finding Inequalities

Activity 1

Draw each of the inequalities on the number lines provided.

1. $a > 10$

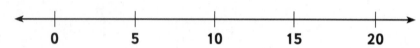

2. $c \geq 71$

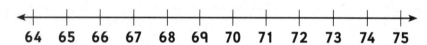

3. $b < -5$

4. $d \leq 189$

Name _____ Date _____

Apply Skills
Using ≥ and ≤

Activity 1

Translate each word statement into an inequality. Write a statement that describes the inequality, then draw the inequality on the number line.

1. The low temperature of the day was at least 25 degrees.

    The variable _____ represents _____ .

    The inequality is _____.

    Statement _____

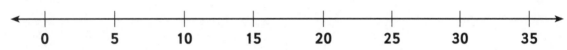

2. The lowest price for airline tickets from Dallas to San Diego for the year was $208.

    The variable _____ represents _____ .

    The inequality is _____.

    Statement _____

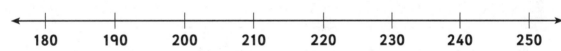

3. Rachel weighs at least as much as Monica. Monica weighs 105 pounds.

    The variable _____ represents _____ .

    The inequality is _____.

    Statement _____

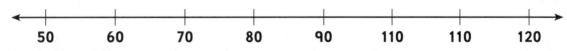

4. Scott is at most 6 feet tall.

    The variable _____ represents _____ .

    The inequality is _____.

    Statement _____

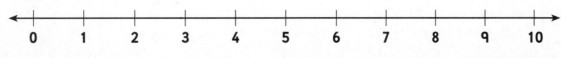

Name _____ Date _____

Activity 2

Look at the inequalities. For each inequality, write a situation that could be described by the inequality.

1. $a > 10$, where a represents the age of a person (in years).

   _____

   _____

   _____

2. $t < 50$, where t represents the temperature (in degrees) outside.

   _____

   _____

   _____

3. $n \geq 25$, where n represents the number of people at the concert.

   _____

   _____

4. $w \leq 100$, where w represents the number of women in the audience.

   _____

   _____

   _____

mBook Reinforce Understanding
Use the mBook *Study Guide* to review lesson concepts.

Name _____ Date _____

 Skills Maintenance
Simplifying Ratios

Activity 1

Simplify the ratios.

Model	$\dfrac{4}{8}$ $\dfrac{1}{2}$

1. $\dfrac{5}{10}$ _____

2. $\dfrac{3}{12}$ _____

3. $\dfrac{8}{24}$ _____

4. $\dfrac{6}{30}$ _____

5. $\dfrac{7}{21}$ _____

6. $\dfrac{6}{24}$ _____

7. $\dfrac{2}{32}$ _____

8. $\dfrac{25}{50}$ _____

9. $\dfrac{14}{49}$ _____

10. $\dfrac{36}{81}$ _____

11. $\dfrac{33}{121}$ _____

12. $\dfrac{4}{36}$ _____

Name _____ Date _____

Problem-Solving Activity
Solving Word Problems Using Unit Rates

Solve the unit rate problems by making and completing the proportions.

1. If milk is 6 cartons for $3.60, how much is just one carton?

    Proportion:

    _____

    The cost for just 1 carton of milk is _____.

2. If you drive 420 miles in 7 hours, how many miles do you drive in just one hour?

    Proportion:

    _____

    How many miles do you drive in an hour? _____

3. If apples are 5 for $2.00, how much is just one?

    Proportion:

    _____

    The cost for just 1 apple is _____.

4. If you can go on 5 rides for 25 tickets, how many tickets for just one ride?

    Proportion:

    _____

    The number of tickets for just one ride is _____.

Name _____ Date _____

Problem-Solving Activity
Solving Word Problems Using Unit Rates

Examine the special pricing situations and determine the better deal by finding the unit rate. Set up the proportion for a quantity of one, then complete the proportion.

1. Hal's Grocery sells apples 12 for $2.40. If it costs $0.25 for 1 apple, is 12 for $2.40 the better deal?

   _____

2. Nature's Snax sells fruit snacks by the pouch for $0.50 or in a 12–pack for $5.00. Which is the better price?

   _____

3. Natalie's school is selling raffle tickets as a fund-raiser. There are 2 packets of tickets you can buy. You can buy 10 tickets for $10 or you can buy 4 tickets for $5.00. Which is the better deal?

   _____

4. Suppose you can buy sugarless gum in a pack of 10 sticks for 80 cents. Another pack of sugarless gum comes in a pack of 20 for $1.00. Which pack of gum is the better deal?

   _____

mBook Reinforce Understanding
Use the mBook *Study Guide* to review lesson concepts.

Name _____ Date _____

Skills Maintenance
Inequalities

Activity 1

Select the inequality that best represents each of the word statements.

1. The temperature will be no higher than 50 today. If t is the temperature:

   (a) $t > 50$

   (b) $t < 50$

   (c) $t \leq 50$

2. Melissa is younger than Michael. Michael is 10. If m is Melissa's age:

   (a) $m < 10$

   (b) $m > 10$

   (c) $m \geq 10$

3. It takes Laci at least 20 minutes to get ready for school in the morning. If t is the time it takes Laci to get ready:

   (a) $t > 20$

   (b) $t \geq 20$

   (c) $t \leq 20$

4. Jamal scored more goals than anyone on the team this year. He scored 15. Micah scored the second highest number of goals. If m represents the number of goals that Micah scored:

   (a) $m \leq 15$

   (b) $m < 15$

   (c) $m > 15$

Name _____ Date _____

 Apply Skills
Logic and Number Lines

> **Activity 1**

Fill in the inequality symbol that represents the inequalities. Then fill in two number lines that show the logic of the inequalities.

1. Amusing Amusements is a park consisting only of roller coasters. The largest roller coaster in the park, the Maniac, has the requirement that you must be at least 12 years old and over 5 feet tall. Complete the inequalities if *A* represents age and *H* represents height.

   A _____ 12 years old

   H _____ 5 feet tall

   Number line showing age requirement:

   ←——————————————————————————→

   Number line showing height requirement:

   ←——————————————————————————→

2. A popular game at the fair is one where you throw baseballs at milk bottles and try to knock them over. When you knock over 10 bottles, you get a prize. There is one catch, though; you have to do it in less than a minute. Complete the inequalities if *b* represents the number of bottles and *t* represents time.

   b _____ 10 bottles

   t _____ 1 minute

   Number line showing the number of bottles you must knock down:

   ←——————————————————————————→

   Number line showing the time restriction:

   ←——————————————————————————→

Name _____ Date _____

3. In order to get a driver's license in a particular state, you must be at least 16 years of age and you must complete at least 50 hours of certified practice driving. Complete the inequalities if *a* represents the age requirement and *h* represents the number of hours of practice driving.

   a _____ 16 years old

   h _____ 50 hours

   Number line showing age requirement:

   Number line showing the requirement for practice driving:

4. A person who rides a horse for a living is called a jockey. There are strict height and weight requirements for jockeys. You must be no more than 62 inches tall and you must weigh less than 120 pounds. Complete the inequalities if *h* represents the height requirement and *w* represents the weight requirement.

   h _____ 62 inches

   w _____ 120 pounds

   Number line showing height requirement:

   Number line showing weight requirement:

mBook **Reinforce Understanding**
Use the mBook *Study Guide* to review lesson concepts.

Name _____ Date _____

Skills Maintenance
Inequalities on the Number Line

Activity 1

Draw each of the inequalities on the number line.

1. $99 \geq x$

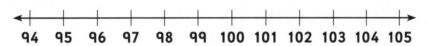

2. $y > 80$

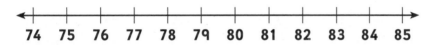

3. $z < 133$

Simplifying Fractions

Activity 2

Simplify the fractions and proportions.

1. $\frac{5}{10}$ _____

2. $\frac{3}{6}$ _____

3. $\frac{6}{8}$ _____

4. $\frac{360 \text{ miles}}{6 \text{ hours}}$ _____

5. $\frac{12}{18}$ _____

Name _____ Date _____

 ## Problem-Solving Activity
Simplifying Rates

Circle the proportions that need to be simplified. Then simplify the proportion and write the new proportion on the blank lines below the table.

1	2	3	4	5
$\frac{8}{12} = \frac{4}{x}$	$\frac{6}{8} = \frac{12}{y}$	$\frac{7}{14} = \frac{x}{16}$	$\frac{10}{12} = \frac{15}{y}$	$\frac{9}{10} = \frac{x}{20}$

1. _____

2. _____

3. _____

4. _____

5. _____

Simplify the rates and solve the problems.

1. Kelly bought 6 headbands for $9. She wants to buy 4 more. How much will it cost to buy 4 headbands?

   Simplify _____ Answer _____

2. Larry bought 8 bags of doggy treats for his pets and it cost him $20. He wants to buy 6 more bags of doggy treats. How much does it cost for 6 bags?

   Simplify _____ Answer _____

3. The day after Thanksgiving, the largest department store in town had a sale on clothing. You could buy 8 pairs of socks for $12. Jenine wanted to 10 pairs of socks. How much will she pay for 10 pairs?

   Simplify _____ Answer _____

4. Huey works for a company that ships products around the world. He loads boxes on a truck. He can stack 12 large boxes on the truck in 15 minutes using a forklift. How many boxes can he stack on the truck in 20 minutes?

   Simplify _____ Answer _____

mBook Reinforce Understanding
Use the mBook *Study Guide* to review lesson concepts.

Name _____ Date _____

Skills Maintenance
Inequalities

Activity 1

Draw the inequalities on the number lines below.

1. $-5 < x$

2. $77 \leq y$

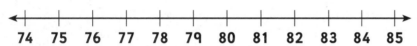

3. $z < 125$

Rate

Activity 2

Simplify and solve the rate problems.

1. 6 bags of chips for $8, 9 bags for x

_____

$x =$ _____

2. 6 bottles of cola for $4, 8 bottles for y

_____

$y =$ _____

3. 3 loaves of bread for $3, 1 loaf for z

_____

$z =$ _____

Name _____ Date _____

%÷ Apply Skills
Double Inequalities

Activity 1

Write double inequalities. Then draw them on a number line.

Model	$x < 5$ and $x > 0$ The double inequality is $0 < x < 5$. On a number line, the inequality looks like this:

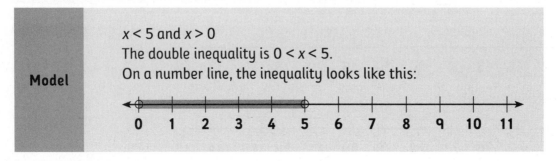

1. $10 > x$ and $x > 4$ The double inequality is _____ .

   On a number line, the inequality looks like this:

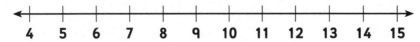

2. $x < 100$ and $x > 50$ The double inequality is _____.

   On a number line, the inequality looks like this:

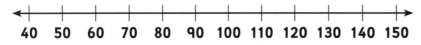

3. $125 \geq x$ and $118 \leq x$ The double inequality is _____.

   On a number line, the inequality looks like this:

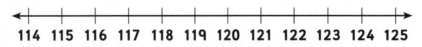

4. $x > 70$ and $x \leq 120$ The double inequality is _____.

   On a number line, the inequality looks like this:

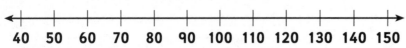

5. $x \geq 220$ and $x < 330$ The double inequality is _____.

   On a number line, the inequality looks like this:

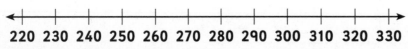

Name _____ Date _____

 Problem-Solving Activity
Using Inequalities in the Real World

Look at the general number and word statements that use double inequalities. For each problem, write a sentence that represents a situation that could be described with the general statement. Then show the inequality on a number line.

1. $125 < m < 365$, where m represents money in dollars

_____

_____

_____

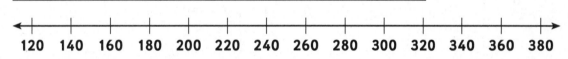

2. $5 \leq w < 15$, where w represents work hours

_____

_____

_____

3. $45 > b \geq 25$, where b represents number of boys

_____

_____

_____

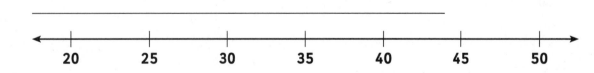

 Reinforce Understanding
Use the mBook *Study Guide* to review lesson concepts.

Name _____ Date _____

 Skills Maintenance
Double Inequalities

Select the double inequality that matches the word statement in each problem.

1. The low temperature for the day was −5 and the high temperature was 15. Show the temperature range, *t*, using a double inequality.

    (a) $-5 \le t \le 15$

    (b) $-5 \le t < 15$

    (c) $-5 < t \le 15$

2. Children in Kiddy's Fun Play Land must be at least 2 and less than 8 years old. Show the range of ages, *a*, using a double inequality.

    (a) $2 < a < 8$

    (b) $2 < a \le 8$

    (c) $2 \le a < 8$

3. The range of scores on the midterm exam went from a low of 53 to a high of 99. Show the range of scores, *s*, using a double inequality.

    (a) $53 < s < 99$

    (b) $53 \le s \le 99$

    (c) $53 > s < 99$

4. At the family reunion, the youngest grandchild was 5 years old and the oldest grandparent was 87. Show the range of ages, *a*, using a double inequality.

    (a) $5 \le a < 87$

    (b) $5 \le a \le 87$

    (c) $5 \le a > 87$

Name _____ Date _____

 Problem-Solving Activity
Comparing Different Rates

Answer the questions by comparing the different rates. Use a proportion to explain your answer.

1. Crew A makes 30 sandwiches in 20 minutes. Crew B makes 50 sandwiches in 30 minutes. Which is the fastest crew? Base the comparison on how many sandwiches they each make in an hour (60 minutes).

   Crew A $\dfrac{\text{Sandwiches}}{\text{Minutes}}$ ___   ___

   Crew B $\dfrac{\text{Sandwiches}}{\text{Minutes}}$ ___   ___

   Which crew is faster? _____

2. Crew C can make 5 signs in 10 minutes. Crew D can make 8 signs in 15 minutes. Which is the fastest crew? Base your decision on how many signs each crew makes in a half hour.

   Crew C $\dfrac{\text{Signs}}{\text{Minutes}}$ ___   ___

   Crew D $\dfrac{\text{Signs}}{\text{Minutes}}$ ___   ___

   Which crew is faster? _____

3. Crew E earns $100 in 3 days. Crew F can earn $150 in 4 days. Which crew earns the most money? Base your decision on 12 days.

   Crew E   Money $\dfrac{\text{Earned}}{\text{Days}}$ _____   _____

   Crew F   Money $\dfrac{\text{Earned}}{\text{Days}}$ _____   _____

   Which crew earns the most money? _____

Unit 3

Name _____ Date _____

 Problem-Solving Activity
Comparing Different Rates

Use what you know about rate problems to answer the questions. Then underline what the question is asking you to find.

1. The Last Stop Car Wash does the cheapest oil changes in town. Andre and Jose are the only two workers on there on Saturday, so there is a long line for oil changes. It takes Andre 40 minutes to change the oil on 2 cars. Jose can do 4 cars in 60 minutes. After 2 hours or 120 minutes, they both take a break. What is the difference in the number of oil changes for the two workers?

    _____

2. Farmers harvest wheat with combines. The newer combines can do the job faster than old combines. A new combine can harvest 30 rows of wheat in 2 hours. The slower, older combine can do just 18 rows of wheat in the same time. What is the difference in the number of rows of wheat after 8 hours?

    _____

3. Let's say that you are driving 50 miles per hour and a car in the fast last goes past you at the rate of 60 miles an hour. How far ahead of you will this car be after 5 hours?

    _____

4. There is usually a big difference between what someone who has been on the job for a long time can do and what a new worker can do. Steele's furniture store puts together cabinets that come from the factory in boxes. Jennice has been working at Steele's for 3 years. She can assemble 15 cabinets in a day. Kara was just hired. She has to keep reading instructions so that she can put together a cabinet. She can only assemble 8 cabinets in a day. What is the difference in the number of cabinets that they can assemble in 5 days?

    _____

mBook Reinforce Understanding
Use the mBook *Study Guide* to review lesson concepts.

Name _____ Date _____

 Skills Maintenance
Solving Rate Problems

Activity 1

Solve the rate problems by completing the proportions.

1. Crew A can stuff 20 envelopes in 5 minutes. Crew B can stuff
    25 envelopes in 15 minutes. Compare their work after 30 minutes.

    Crew A $\dfrac{\text{Envelopes}}{\text{Minutes}}$ $\dfrac{20}{5}$ $\dfrac{}{30}$

    Crew B $\dfrac{\text{Envelopes}}{\text{Minutes}}$ $\dfrac{25}{15}$ $\dfrac{}{30}$

    Which crew is faster? _____

2. Crew A can frost 15 cupcakes in 20 minutes. Crew B can frost
    5 cupcakes in 5 minutes. Compare their work after 60 minutes.

    Crew A $\dfrac{\text{Cupcakes}}{\text{Minutes}}$ $\dfrac{15}{20}$ $\dfrac{}{60}$

    Crew B $\dfrac{\text{Cupcakes}}{\text{Minutes}}$ $\dfrac{5}{5}$ $\dfrac{}{60}$

    Which crew is faster? _____

3. Crew A can wash 10 windows in 15 minutes. Crew B can wash
    15 windows in 20 minutes. Compare their work after 60 minutes.

    Crew A $\dfrac{\text{Windows}}{\text{Minutes}}$ $\dfrac{10}{15}$ $\dfrac{}{60}$

    Crew B $\dfrac{\text{Windows}}{\text{Minutes}}$ $\dfrac{15}{20}$ $\dfrac{}{60}$

    Which crew is faster? _____

Name _____ Date _____

%÷= <x Apply Skills
Showing the Range on a Number Line

Activity 1

For each of the problems, show the two ranges of values that are possible answers for the inequality on the number line.

1. $5 < x < 10$ and $x > 12$

2. $-1 \leq y < 3$ and $y \geq 5$

3. $20 \leq x \leq 40$ and $x > 60$

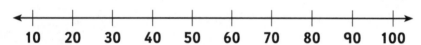

Activity 2

Tell if the number is within the range of possible values. Circle True or False.

1. $5 < x < 11$ and $x > 25$

    10 is in the range of the values   True   or   False

2. $-4 < y < 4$ and $y > 10$

    4 is in the range of the values   True   or   False

3. $2 \leq w < 12$ and $w > 21$

    12 is in the range of the values   True   or   False

4. $0 \leq z \leq 5$ and $z \geq 10$

    5 is in the range of the values   True   or   False

5. $15 < x \leq 25$ and $x \geq 30$

    35 is in the range of the values   True   or   False

mBook Reinforce Understanding
Use the mBook *Study Guide* to review lesson concepts.

Name _____ Date _____

Skills Maintenance
Inequalities

Activity 1

Select the inequality that best represents each of the word statements.

1. Alicia is at least 12 years old. If a is Alicia's age:

   (a) $12 > a$

   (b) $a \leq 12$

   (c) $a \geq 12$

2. The temperature today will not be above 50. If t is the temperature:

   (a) $t \leq 50$

   (b) $t \geq 50$

   (c) $t < 50$

3. Becca got a 95 on her last test. Lisa was the only one to get a higher score. If l is Lisa's score:

   (a) $l \leq 95$

   (b) $l > 95$

   (c) $l \geq 95$

4. Michael is younger than Blake. Blake is 15. If m represents Michael's age:

   (a) $m < 15$

   (b) $m \leq 15$

   (c) $m \geq 15$

Unit 3

Name _____ Date _____

Unit Review
Inequalities

Activity 1

Tell whether each of the statements is True or False. Circle the correct answer.

Model	If $x > 5$, a possible value of x is 2. True or (False)

1. If $x < 17$, a possible value of x is 20.

   True   or   False

2. If $3 > y$, a possible value of y is 3.

   True   or   False

3. If $w \leq 3$, a possible value of w is 3.

   True   or   False

4. If $z \geq 125$, a possible value of z is 100.

   True   or   False

5. If $40 \leq A \geq 60$, a possible value of A is 40.

   True   or   False

6. If $103 \leq m$, a possible value of m is 104.

   True   or   False

Name _____ Date _____

Activity 2

Write inequalities based on the word problems. Then draw the inequalities on the number lines.

1. Jenny runs a volunteer program after school. She has about 50 volunteers, but needs to know how old they are so she can assign them to specific activities. Jenny figures out that most of the volunteers are from 15 to 22 years old or from 40 to 60 years old.

_____

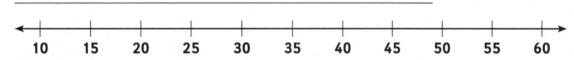

2. Ralph is ordering a shipment of peppers for his restaurant. He needs to find a ballpark number for how many peppers people eat a week. When he looks at his lists, he sees that in Week 1, 106 peppers were eaten, and in Week 2, 53 peppers were eaten.

_____

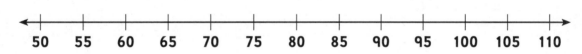

3. You're about to study to take your final exam in math. You want to find a ballpark range of hours to study, so you ask the people who have scored the highest on previous tests how many hours they studied. You find that the people who scored the highest studied between 7 and 15 hours.

_____

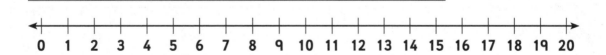

Name _____ Date _____

Activity 3

These problems require you to create different kinds of number lines. Make sure that you think about the scale for the number line before you draw it. Some of the problems only use one range of values. Other problems require you to show more than one range of values for a variable.

1. Copper melts at 1,985 degrees. Stainless steel melts at 2,600 degrees. Cast iron melts at a temperature greater than copper and less than stainless steel. Let j = the temperature that cast iron melts.

2. Ms. Fanning's social studies class just took a big test. After grading the test, Ms. Fanning told the class, "You either did very well or very poorly on the test. If you did poorly, you'll have to take a make-up test. The scores on the test were either below 65 or above 90." Let x = the grades on the test.

3. Jana Cooper is practicing for the 100-meter dash. During practice today, she ran the 100 meters 8 times. Her fastest time was 11.5 seconds and her slowest time was 14.5 seconds. All of her other runs were in between these two times. Let r = the different times that Jana ran in practice today.

4. Commercial airlines fly at different altitudes in order to avoid rough weather and so that they are at a different altitude than planes flying in another direction. Flight 448 from Boston to Miami flew part of the way between 28,000 and 32,000 feet and the rest of the way from 35,000 to 38,000 feet. Let p = the flying altitude of Flight 448.

Name _____ Date _____

Unit Review
Working With Rates

Activity 1

Complete the proportions to find the unit rates.

1. 10 apples for $4.00. The unit rate is:

    $\dfrac{\text{Number of apples}}{\text{Cost}}$ $\dfrac{10}{\$4} = \dfrac{1}{x}$

    How much for one apple? _____

2. 15 packs of fruit snacks for $3.00. The unit rate is:

    $\dfrac{\text{Number of packs}}{\text{Cost}}$ $\dfrac{15}{\$3} = \dfrac{1}{y}$

    How much for one pack of fruit snacks? _____

3. 3 pairs of jeans for $150. The unit rate is:

    $\dfrac{\text{Number of pairs of jeans}}{\text{Cost}}$ $\dfrac{3}{\$150} = \dfrac{1}{a}$

    How much for one pair of jeans? _____

4. 2 CDs cost $40. The unit rate is:

    $\dfrac{\text{Number of CDs}}{\text{Cost}}$ $\dfrac{2}{\$40} = \dfrac{1}{b}$

    How much for one CD? _____

Name _____ Date _____

Activity 2

Read the word problems and find the difference in rates. Remember, these problems require more than setting up a proportion.

1. Angie can read a chapter in her textbook in half an hour. It takes Laurie 45 minutes to read the same amount. If they both read 3 chapters in their textbook, how much longer will it take Laurie?

    _____

2. Colin and Matt are taking a day off from work to go snowboarding. They decide to split up and see who can snowboard down the mountain the most times. Colin can get down the mountain 5 times in an hour and a half. Matt can get down the mountain 3 times in an hour. If they spend 6 hours at the mountain, who will have snowboarded down the mountain the most?

    _____

3. It is election day, and the polls are expecting very large crowds. Poll A records that 450 people vote per hour. Poll B reports that 400 people vote every 45 minutes. At the end of 12 hours, how many more people voted at Poll B?

    _____

mBook **Reinforce Understanding**
Use the mBook *Study Guide* to review lesson concepts.

Name _____ Date _____

Skills Maintenance
Patterns

Activity 1

Fill in the missing numbers in each of the patterns.

Model	100, 90, __80__ , 70, 60, __50__ , __40__

1. 2, _____ , 6, _____ , 10, 12, 14, _____ , _____

2. _____ , 6, 9, _____ , 15, _____ , 21, 24, 27

3. 75, 70, 65, _____ , 55, _____ , _____ , 40, _____

4. 7, 12, 17, 22, _____ , _____ , 37, 42, _____ , 52

5. 800, 700, _____ , 500, _____ , 300, 200, _____

6. 119, 121, _____ , 125, 127, _____ , 131, _____

Name _____ Date _____

Apply Skills
Algebraic Patterns

Activity 1

Write the algebraic pattern using variables. Then tell how many circles there will be in a certain box in the pattern.

1. What is the algebraic pattern shown below? _____

   How many circles will there be in the 15th box? _____

Box 1	Box 2	Box 3	Box 4	Box 5
o	oo	ooo	oooo	ooooo

2. What is the algebraic pattern shown below? _____

   How many circles will there be in the 10th box? _____

Box 1	Box 2	Box 3	Box 4	Box 5
ooo	oooooo	ooooooooo	oooooooooooo	ooooooooooooooo

3. What is the algebraic pattern shown below? _____

   How many circles will there be in the 9th box? _____

Box 1	Box 2	Box 3	Box 4	Box 5
oooo	oooooooo	oooooooooooo	oooooooooooooooo	oooooooooooooooooooo

4. What is the algebraic pattern shown below? _____

   How many circles will there be in the 8th box? _____

Box 1	Box 2	Box 3	Box 4	Box 5
ooooo	oooooooooo	ooooooooooooooo	oooooooooooooooooooo	ooooooooooooooooooooooooo

Name _____ Date _____

Problem-Solving Activity
Another Way to Show Ratios

Use the information to create as many different ratios as you can. Make
sure you do these things:

- Write each ratio in horizontal form,
- Write a statement that describes the ratio,
- Tell if the ratio is a part-to-part or part-to-whole relationship.

Model	Miguel's baseball team has five right-handed pitchers and two left-handed pitchers. There are 25 players on the team. 5 : 2 "5 right-handed pitchers to 2 left-handed pitchers" part-to-part ratio 5 : 25 "5 right-handed pitchers to 25 players" part-to-whole ratio 2 : 25 "2 left-handed pitchers to 25 players" part-to-whole ratio

1. Marcus works at the company that makes phonebooks. There are two parts to the phonebook—the white pages and the yellow pages. There are 275 white pages and 320 yellow pages in a phonebook that is 595 pages long.

   _____

   _____

   _____

2. There are three kinds of seats still left for the next professional basketball playoff game. There are 75 cheap seats, 40 average price seats, and 85 expensive seats left for a total of 200 seats that are not sold for the game.

   _____

   _____

   _____

   _____

   _____

   _____

Name _____ Date _____

 ### Skills Maintenance
Algebraic Patterns

Activity 1

Select the set of boxes that represents the algebraic pattern. The variable *n* represents the box number.

1. $5 \cdot n$

(a)

Box 1	Box 2	Box 3	Box 4
OOOOO	OOOO	OOO	OO

(b)

Box 1	Box 2	Box 3	Box 4
OO	OOOO	OOOOOO	OOOO OOOO OOOO OOOO

(c)

Box 1	Box 2	Box 3	Box 4
OOOOO	OOOOO OOOOO	OOOOO OOOOO OOOOO	OOOOO OOOOO OOOOO OOOOO

2. $n \cdot 3$

(a)

Box 1	Box 2	Box 3	Box 4
	O	OO	OOO

(b)

Box 1	Box 2	Box 3	Box 4
OOO	OOOOOO	OOOOOO OOO	OOOOOO OOOOOO

(c)

Box 1	Box 2	Box 3	Box 4
OOOO	OOO	OO	O

Name _____ Date _____

3. $10 \cdot n$

(a)

Box 1	Box 2	Box 3	Box 4
○○○○○ ○○○○○	○○○○○ ○○○○○ ○○○○○ ○○○○○	○○○○○ ○○○○○ ○○○○○ ○○○○○ ○○○○○ ○○○○○	○○○○○ ○○○○○ ○○○○○ ○○○○○ ○○○○○ ○○○○○ ○○○○○ ○○○○○

(b)

Box 1	Box 2	Box 3	Box 4
○○○	○○○○	○○○○○	○○○○○○

(c)

Box 1	Box 2	Box 3	Box 4
○○○○○ ○○○○○	○○○○ ○○○○	○○○○○○	○○○○

Name _____ Date _____

 ### Problem-Solving Activity
Comparing Ratios

Look at the pairs of ratios in the problems. Cross out the ratio that needs to be changed so you can compare the two ratios. Then write the equivalent ratio. Circle what is the same in the pair of ratios—cost or quantity.

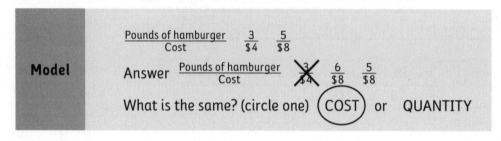

Model	$\dfrac{\text{Pounds of hamburger}}{\text{Cost}}$ $\dfrac{3}{\$4}$ $\dfrac{5}{\$8}$
	Answer $\dfrac{\text{Pounds of hamburger}}{\text{Cost}}$ $\cancel{\dfrac{3}{\$4}}$ $\dfrac{6}{\$8}$ $\dfrac{5}{\$8}$
	What is the same? (circle one) (COST) or QUANTITY

1. $\dfrac{\text{sweaters}}{\text{cost}}$ $\dfrac{3}{\$18}$ $\dfrac{5}{\$36}$

   What is the same? (circle one)   COST   or   QUANTITY

2. $\dfrac{\text{dozen muffins}}{\text{cost}}$ $\dfrac{4}{\$15}$ $\dfrac{8}{\$25}$

   What is the same? (circle one)   COST   or   QUANTITY

3. $\dfrac{\text{pairs of jeans}}{\text{cost}}$ $\dfrac{6}{\$100}$ $\dfrac{3}{\$40}$

   What is the same? (circle one)   COST   or   QUANTITY

Name _____ Date _____

4. $\dfrac{\text{apples}}{\text{cost}}$ $\dfrac{12}{\$6}$ $\dfrac{24}{\$10}$

   What is the same? (circle one)   COST   or   QUANTITY

5. $\dfrac{\text{pairs of shoes}}{\text{cost}}$ $\dfrac{4}{\$120}$ $\dfrac{2}{\$80}$

   What is the same? (circle one)   COST   or   QUANTITY

6. $\dfrac{\text{soft drinks}}{\text{cost}}$ $\dfrac{6\text{ pack}}{\$2}$ $\dfrac{8\text{ pack}}{\$6}$

   What is the same? (circle one)   COST   or   QUANTITY

mBook Reinforce Understanding
Use the mBook *Study Guide* to review lesson concepts.

Name _____ Date _____

Skills Maintenance
Equivalent Ratios

Activity 1

Look at the pairs of ratios in the problems. Cross out the ratio that needs to be changed so you can compare the two ratios. Then write the equivalent ratio. Circle what is the same in each ratio—the cost or the quantity.

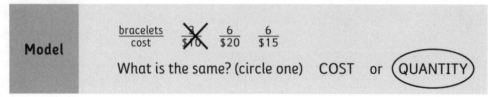

Model	$\dfrac{bracelets}{cost}$ $\cancel{\dfrac{3}{\$10}}$ $\dfrac{6}{\$20}$ $\dfrac{6}{\$15}$
	What is the same? (circle one) COST or (QUANTITY)

1. $\dfrac{packs\ of\ gum}{cost}$ $\dfrac{3}{\$2}$ $\dfrac{4}{\$4}$

   What is the same? (circle one)   COST   or   QUANTITY

2. bags of chips $\dfrac{4}{\$12}$ $\dfrac{2}{\$5}$

   What is the same? (circle one)   COST   or   QUANTITY

3. $\dfrac{colas}{cost}$ $\dfrac{6\ pack}{\$3}$ $\dfrac{8\ pack}{\$6}$

   What is the same? (circle one)   COST   or   QUANTITY

Name _____ Date _____

Apply Skills
Complex Patterns

Activity 1

Make a table to find the algebraic pattern. Then use the pattern to tell how many circles are in a particular box.

1.

Box 1	Box 2	Box 3	Box 4	Box 5
OOOO	OOOOO	OOOOOO	OOOOOOO	OOOO OOOO

(a) Transfer the pattern to a table.

(b) Analyze the pattern in the table and write the algebraic pattern. _____

(c) How many circles are in the 10th box? _____

2.

Box 1	Box 2	Box 3	Box 4	Box 5
OOOOO	OOOOOO	OOOO OOO	OOOO OOOO	OOOOO OOOO

(a) Transfer the pattern to a table.

(b) Analyze the pattern in the table and write the algebraic pattern. _____

(c) How many circles are in the 20th box? _____

Name _____ Date _____

3.

Box 1	Box 2	Box 3	Box 4	Box 5
○○○○○ ○○○○○ ○	○○○○○ ○○○○○ ○○	○○○○○ ○○○○○ ○○○	○○○○○ ○○○○○ ○○○○	○○○○○ ○○○○○ ○○○○○

(a) Transfer the pattern to a table.

(b) Analyze the pattern in the table and write the algebraic pattern. _____

(c) How many circles are in the 100th box? _____

4.

Box 1	Box 2	Box 3	Box 4	Box 5
○○○○○ ○○○○○ ○○○○○ ○○○○○ ○	○○○○○ ○○○○○ ○○○○○ ○○○○○ ○○	○○○○○ ○○○○○ ○○○○○ ○○○○○ ○○○	○○○○○ ○○○○○ ○○○○○ ○○○○○ ○○○○	○○○○○ ○○○○○ ○○○○○ ○○○○○ ○○○○○

(a) Transfer the pattern to a table.

(b) Analyze the pattern in the table and write the algebraic pattern. _____

(c) How many circles are in the 200th box? _____

Name _____ Date _____

Problem-Solving Activity
Rounding and Ratios

Look at the sale prices. Use what you know about rounding to the nearest whole number to make comparisons. Find the equivalent ratio to make comparing easier, then substitute the new ratio to make the comparison using colons. Show your work.

Al's One-Day Bakery Sale	
3 pies for $4.59	6 pies for $7.99
12 donuts for $4.79	36 donuts for $12.25
2 loaves of bread for $4.20	6 loaves of bread for $15.60
6 cupcakes for $2.10	20 cupcakes for 5.89
2 cakes for $6.99	?

1. What is the best deal on pies? _____

2. What is the best deal on bread? _____

3. What is the best deal on cupcakes? _____

4. Write a ratio for five cakes that is a better deal than two cakes for $6.99.

Name _____ Date _____

 Skills Maintenance
Complex Patterns

Activity 1

Select the algebraic pattern that matches the pattern of the numbers in the table.

1.

Box Number	1	2	3	4	5
Circles	2	3	4	5	6

(a) $n - 1$

(b) $n + 2$

(c) $n + 1$

2.

Box Number	1	2	3	4	5
Circles	4	5	6	7	8

(a) $n - 3$

(b) $n + 3$

(c) $n + 4$

3.

Box Number	1	2	3	4	5
Circles	0	1	2	3	4

(a) $n - 1$

(b) $n + 0$

(c) $n + 1$

Name _____ Date _____

 Problem-Solving Activity
Ratio Problems

The table shows the costs for different items in a discount drug store.
Find the ratio or proportion to answer the questions, based on the
information in the table. Show your work.

Sammie's Discount Drugstore		
Item	**Quantity and Price**	**Weekly Special**
Soap	10 bars for $4	no
Razors	5 razors for $5	10 razors for $8
Hair bands	1 box for $3.00	no
Combs	3 combs for $1	no
Toothpaste	4 tubes for $8	7 tubes for $16
Toothbrush	2 toothbrushes $6	no
Shampoo	2 bottles for $5	8 bottles $20
Bandages	4 boxes for $8	no

1. You want to buy toothpaste. Which is the better deal, the regular
   price or the sale price? _____

   _____

2. What is the cost of just one bar of soap? _____

   _____

3. How much do you need to pay if you buy 9 combs and
   4 toothbrushes? _____

   _____

4. Which is the better deal on shampoo, the regular price or the
   sale price? _____

   _____

Name _____ Date _____

Skills Maintenance
Types of Ratio Problems

Activity 1

Tell whether the ratios belong to a proportion or unit rate problem.

1. $\dfrac{\text{cookies}}{\text{cost}}$ $\dfrac{25}{\$5} = \dfrac{50}{x}$

   (a) proportion

   (b) unit rate

2. $\dfrac{\text{CDs}}{\text{Cost}}$ $\dfrac{4}{\$5} = \dfrac{1}{x}$

   (a) proportion

   (b) unit rate

3. $\dfrac{\text{bracelets}}{\text{cost}}$ $\dfrac{30}{\$10} = \dfrac{50}{x}$

   (a) proportion

   (b) unit rate

4. $\dfrac{\text{apples}}{\text{cost}}$ $\dfrac{25}{\$5} = \dfrac{1}{x}$

   (a) proportion

   (b) unit rate

Name _____ Date _____

Apply Skills
Patterns in Tessellations

Activity 1

Find the algebraic expression for each of the visual patterns. Complete the tables and use them to help find the pattern.

1. Each colored set of stars makes up a ring in the pattern. The black star in the middle of the pattern does not count as part of the pattern. Start with the five stars in the center ring, and then work outward.

Ring				
Stars				

The algebraic expression is _____.

How many stars are there in the 8th ring of the pattern? _____

Name _____ Date _____

2. The blank X at the center of this pattern does not count as part of the pattern. The first ring involves the four grey squares that go around the blank X. The next ring has eight black squares.

Ring			
Squares			

The algebraic expression is _____.

How many squares are there in the 11ᵗʰ ring of the pattern? _____

3. The black hexagon in the center of this tessellation is not part of the pattern. Start with the first ring of 6 hexagons.

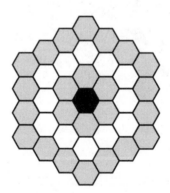

Ring			
Hexagons			

The algebraic expression is _____.

How many hexagons are there on the 6ᵗʰ ring of the tessellation? _____

Name _____ Date _____

4. Start with the four octagons in the center of the pattern.

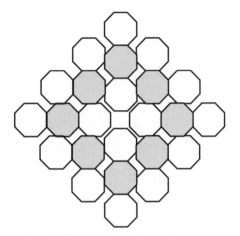

Ring			
Octagons			

The algebraic expression is _____.

How many octagons are there on the 20th ring of the pattern? _____

mBook **Reinforce Understanding**
Use the **mBook** *Study Guide* to review lesson concepts.

Unit 4 • Lesson 5   **145**

Name _____ Date _____

 Skills Maintenance
Finding the Mathematical Operation

Activity 1

Fill in the missing operation in each of the statements.

Model	4 ___+___ 4 = 8

1. 3 _____ 6 = 18

2. 27 _____ 3 = 9

3. 3 _____ 6 = 9

4. 4 _____ 3 = 7

5. 27 _____ 3 = 30

6. 4 _____ 3 = 12

7. 3 _____ 6 = −3

8. 4 _____ 3 = 1

Name _____ Date _____

 **Apply Skills**
Number Machines

Activity 1

Tell what is being done to the input to get the output in each problem.
Write the algebraic expression and fill in the missing numbers.

1.   Number In 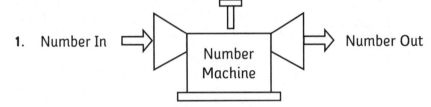 Number Out

In	Out
3	9
40	120
	6
1	

Describe the pattern using words.

_____

Write the pattern using algebra. _____

2.   Number In 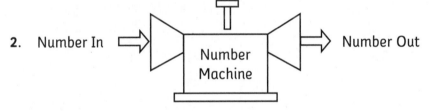 Number Out

In	Out
7	63
10	
	9
9	81

Describe the pattern using words.

_____

Write the pattern using algebra. _____

3.   Number In 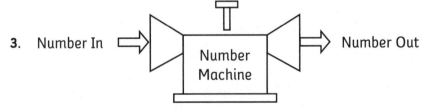 Number Out

In	Out
	32
7	56
8	
80	640

Describe the pattern using words.

_____

Write the pattern using algebra. _____

Name _____ Date _____

4. Number In ⇒ Number Machine ⇒ Number Out

In	Out
	600
20	120
3	18
5	

Describe the pattern using words.

_____

Write the pattern using algebra. _____

5. Number In ⇒ Number Machine ⇒ Number Out

In	Out
612	0
5	0
1	
85	0

Describe the pattern using words.

_____

Write the pattern using algebra. _____

Name _____ Date _____

Problem-Solving Activity
Mixtures

Answer the questions about ratios and percents. Make sure to figure out the difference between the parts and the whole. Remember to find the total amount in a mixture by adding the two parts together.

1. Any soda that you get from a fast food restaurant is a combination of syrup and water. If you want to make a 12-ounce soda, just add three ounces of syrup to water.

   What is the ratio of syrup to the soda? _____

   What percent of the soda is water? _____

2. The workers have to make plaster to fill in the hole in the wall. You make plaster by adding six ounces of water to 12 ounces of powder.

   What is the ratio of water to the plaster mixture? _____

   What percent of the mixture is powder? _____

3. If you want to make pancakes, use flour, sugar, and baking powder. These are called the dry ingredients. You use eight ounces of flour, one ounce of sugar, and one ounce of baking powder to make a small batch of pancakes.

   What is the ratio of sugar to the pancake mixture? _____

   What percent of the mixture is flour? _____

4. A snack mix has raisins, peanuts, cereal, and chocolate candies. Make the mix by adding two cups of raisins, three cups of peanuts, three cups of cereal, and two cups of chocolate candies.

   What is the ratio of cereal to mix? _____

   What is the ratio of peanuts to chocolate candies? _____

   What percent of the mix is raisins? _____

mBook Reinforce Understanding
Use the mBook *Study Guide* to review lesson concepts.

Name _____ Date _____

 Skills Maintenance
Finding the Mathematical Operation

Activity 1

For each of the statements, fill in the missing operation.

Model	4 ___+___ 4 = 8

1. 3 _____ 4 = 12

2. 54 _____ 6 = 9

3. 8 _____ 6 = 14

4. 41 _____ 37 = 4

5. 20 _____ 4 = 5

6. 3 _____ 4 = 7

7. 41 _____ 37 = 78

8. 20 _____ 4 = 16

Name _____ Date _____

 Apply Skills
More Complicated Number Machines

Activity 1

Study the inputs and outputs to decide what operation is being performed
by the number machine. Then write the pattern using algebra.

1. Number In ⟹ [Number Machine] ⟹ Number Out

In	Out
45	5
36	4
1	$\frac{1}{9}$
9	1

Describe the pattern using words.

_____

Write the pattern using algebra. _____

Could this pattern be described using more than one operation?
If so, write the other pattern using algebra. _____

2. Number In ⟹ [Number Machine] ⟹ Number Out

In	Out
50	100
75	125
0.3	50.3
$\frac{1}{2}$	$50\frac{1}{2}$

Describe the pattern using words.

_____

Write the pattern using algebra. _____

Could this pattern be described using more than one operation?
If so, write the other pattern using algebra. _____

Unit 4

Name _____ Date _____

3. Number In ⇨ Number Machine ⇨ Number Out

In	Out
$\frac{4}{5}$	$\frac{4}{10}$
$\frac{1}{8}$	$\frac{1}{16}$
$\frac{1}{2}$	$\frac{1}{4}$
2	1

Describe the pattern using words.

_____

Write the pattern using algebra. _____

Could this pattern be described using more than one operation?
If so, write the other pattern using algebra. _____

4. Number In ⇨ Number Machine ⇨ Number Out

In	Out
500	250
275	25
300	50
1,000	750

Describe the pattern using words.

_____

Write the pattern using algebra. _____

Could this pattern be described using more than one operation?
If so, write the other pattern using algebra. _____

5. Number In ⇨ Number Machine ⇨ Number Out

In	Out
5	5
$\frac{1}{5}$	$\frac{1}{5}$
4.5	4.5
234	234

Describe the pattern using words.

_____

Write the pattern using algebra. _____

Could this pattern be described using more than one operation?
If so, write the other pattern using algebra.

_____

Name _____ Date _____

Problem-Solving Activity
Simple Experiments

Fill in the ratio tables to help figure out the right amounts for each experiment. Answer the questions about percents. Remember that we can only find percents when we have a part-to-whole relationship.

1. You can make a volcano using vinegar and baking soda. First you need to make the volcano cone. You do that by using the following ingredients.

   12 cups flour

   4 cups salt

   4 cups water

   You mix all of this together to make the cone. Let's say that you want to make a cone that is two times as big.

   What is the amount of flour, salt, and water that you need for the cone?

   _____

   What is the ratio of flour to the total mixture? _____

   What percent of the total mixture is water? _____

2. You can make a bouncing ball out of four ingredients. Here is what you need:

   1 part borax soap

   6 parts water

   3 parts white glue

   2 parts corn starch

   To make the ball, you have to mix the soap and water together first. Then you add the glue and cornstarch. Let's say you wanted to make a large ball. You want one that is 4 times as big. Use a ratio table to figure all of the right amounts.

   What is the ratio of corn starch to water? _____

   What percent of the mixture is glue? _____

Name _____ Date _____

3. You can make your own ice cream using a large and a small can. Put the ingredients inside the small can, and put the small can inside of a large can. Then pack ice and rock salt around the small can. Here are the ingredients for ice cream:

1 cup sugar

2 cups milk

2 cups whipping cream

What is the ratio of milk to whipping cream? _____

What percent of the mixture is sugar? _____

What percent of the mixture is milk? _____

If you wanted to make a mixture that had 6 cups of milk, how much sugar would you need? _____

How many cups would be in the total mixture if you made a mixture that had 6 cups of milk? _____

mBook Reinforce Understanding
Use the mBook *Study Guide* to review lesson concepts.

Name _____ Date _____

Skills Maintenance
Rational Number Conversions

Activity 1

Fill in the missing parts in the table.

Fraction	Decimal Number	Percent
$\frac{3}{4}$	0.75	
	0.25	25%
$\frac{5}{5}$		100%
$\frac{1}{5}$	0.20	
	0.5	50%
$\frac{4}{5}$		80%
	1.5	150%
$\frac{1}{3}$		33%

Name _____ Date _____

%÷ Apply Skills
Patterns and Types of Numbers

Activity 1

Use algebra to identify the different types of numbers. Show your work.

1. Which numbers work for $2 \cdot n$?

   10 11 12 13 14 15 16 17 18 19 20 21 22

   _____

   _____

   _____

   These are called _____ numbers.

2. Which of the numbers work for $2 \cdot n + 1$?

   10 11 12 13 14 15 16 17 18 19 20 21 22

   _____

   _____

   _____

   These are called _____ numbers.

3. Which of the numbers work for $\frac{n}{n} = 1$ and $\frac{n}{1} = n$, but are not divisible by any other number?

   10 11 12 13 14 15 16 17 18 19 20 21 22

   Show your work here:

   _____

   _____

   _____

   These are called _____ numbers.

Name _____ Date _____

Problem-Solving Activity
Ratios and Percents

Determine which situation has the biggest percent increase. Find the ratios, then convert them to decimal numbers and percents.

1. The people who own buildings in Shanghai, China, are in a race to build the tallest building. The Yang Tower added 40 stories to its original building, which was already 80 stories tall. The Ling Office Complex added 30 stories to its building, which was already 90 stories tall. Which building had the biggest percent increase in height?

    _____

    _____

2. Bethany's softball team had 10 more home runs this year than last year. Last year, her team had 40 home runs. Jalicia's team also had 10 more home runs this year and last year her team had 50 home runs. Which team had a bigger percent increase in home runs?

    _____

    _____

3. This year two farmers did an experiment. Jones put the fertilizer GroTec on his corn. It was 3 feet taller than last year. Last year his corn was 6 feet tall. Marston put Chemrow on his corn. Last year his corn was 5 feet tall. This year it was 2 feet taller. Which fertilizer made the biggest percent increase?

    _____

    _____

4. Jamar bought a smaller car, and he now gets 15 more miles per gallon that his last car did. With his last car, he got 20 miles per gallon. His cousin, Trece, also bought a new car. He gets 20 more miles per gallon. He used to get 30 miles per gallon with his old car. Who got the biggest percent increase in miles per gallon with their new car?

    _____

    _____

Unit 4

Name _____ Date _____

Skills Maintenance
Rational Number Conversions

Activity 1

Fill in the missing parts in the table.

Fraction	Decimal Number	Percent
$\frac{1}{4}$	0.25	
	0.01	1%
$\frac{2}{5}$		40%
$\frac{3}{4}$	0.75	
	0.6	60%
$\frac{1}{8}$		12.5%
	0.001	0.1%
$\frac{4}{8}$		50%

Name _____ Date _____

Apply Skills
More Number Patterns

Activity 1

Use algebra to identify the different divisibility rules. Circle the numbers that apply. Show your work.

1. Which numbers work for $\frac{n}{2}$ and have no remainder?

   10   11   12   13   14   15   16   17   18   19   20   21   22

   _____

   _____

   _____

   This is the divisibility rule for _____

2. Which numbers work for $\frac{n}{3}$ and $\frac{n}{2}$ and have no remainder?

   110   111   112   113   114   115   116   117   118   119   120   121   122

   _____

   _____

   _____

   This is the divisibility rule for _____

3. Which numbers work for $\frac{n}{5}$ and have no remainder?

   510   511   512   513   514   515   516   517   518   519   520   521   522

   _____

   _____

   _____

   This is the divisibility rule for _____

Unit 4

Name _____ Date _____

Problem-Solving Activity
Percent Decrease

Tell which situation had the biggest percent decrease. Find the ratios, then convert them to decimal numbers and percents. Show your work.

1. The sale of homes dropped this year in the Wallington and Sunnyside neighborhoods. Last year, 50 homes were sold in Wallington. This year, 10 fewer homes sold. Last year, 40 homes were sold in the Sunnyside neighborhood. This year, 5 fewer homes sold. Which neighborhood had the biggest percent decrease?

_____

_____

_____

2. Every year, the music industry seems to sell fewer and fewer CDs. This year, they sold 4 million fewer R&B CDs than last year. They also sold 3 million fewer Jazz CDs than last year. They sold 12 million R&B CDs last year and 10 million Jazz CDs this year. Which type of music had the biggest percent decrease?

_____

_____

_____

3. People actually get shorter as they grow old. Tyrell and Lamar are twin brothers. At age 50, Tyrell was 70 inches tall. Lamar was 72 inches tall. By age 60, Tyrell was 68 inches tall and Lamar was 69 inches tall. Which brother had the biggest percent decrease?

_____

_____

_____

mBook Reinforce Understanding
Use the mBook *Study Guide* to review lesson concepts.

Name _____ Date _____

 Skills Maintenance
Rational Number Conversions

Activity 1

Fill in the missing parts in the table.

Fraction	Decimal Number	Percent
$\frac{4}{16}$	0.25	
	0.57	57%
$\frac{3}{15}$		20%
$\frac{2}{10}$	0.20	
	0.77	77%

Patterns

Activity 2

Fill in the missing numbers in each of the patterns.

1. 25, 30, _____, 40, 45, 50, 55, 60, _____

2. _____, 24, 27, _____, 33, 36, 39, _____, 45

3. 6, 8, 10, _____, 14, _____, 18, _____, 22, 24

4. 6, 12, 18, 24, _____, 36, 42, _____, 54

Name _____ Date _____

Unit Review
Algebraic Patterns

Activity 1

Fill in the table that shows how many squares are in each ring of the pattern. Then write algebraic expressions to show the relationship in the table. Find how many squares are on the 6th ring of this pattern.

What is the algebraic expression going out? _____

How many squares are there in the 6th ring? _____

Name _____ Date _____

Activity 2

Write the numbers that go in the missing blanks in the table. Then write the expression that represents the pattern.

1. Number In 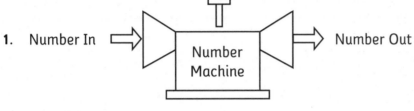 Number Out

   Algebraic expression _____

In	Out
50	41
11	2
23	
15	
83	74

2. Number In 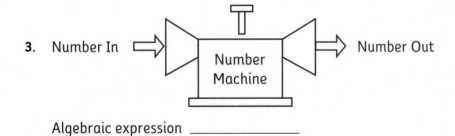 Number Out

   Algebraic expression _____

In	Out
7	35
2	10
20	
1	
15	75

3. Number In Number Machine Number Out

   Algebraic expression _____

In	Out
15	225
8	64
10	
7	
9	81

Unit 4

Name _____ Date _____

Activity 3

Tell what each number is divisible by, according to the divisibility rules you've learned. Then state if the number is even or odd. Tell whether it is prime.

1. 15 _____

2. 23 _____

3. 36 _____

4. 30 _____

5. 14 _____

6. 21 _____

7. 100 _____

8. 41 _____

Name _____ Date _____

Unit 4 Review
Ratios

Activity 1

Select the setup that matches the type of problem asked for. Then explain how you know it's that kind of problem.

1. Which one of these problems is set up as a unit rate problem?

    (a) $\dfrac{\text{Inches}}{\text{miles}}$ $\dfrac{5}{50} = \dfrac{1}{x}$

    (b) $\dfrac{\text{balloons}}{\text{cost}}$ $\dfrac{10}{\$5} = \dfrac{20}{\$7}$

    (c) $\dfrac{\text{bubble gum}}{\text{cost}}$ $\dfrac{5}{\$2} = \dfrac{10}{x}$

    Explain how you know this problem is a unit rate problem.

    _____

    _____

2. Which one of these problems is set up as a proportion problem?

    (a) $\dfrac{\text{Buses}}{\text{students}}$ $\dfrac{2}{24} = \dfrac{1}{a}$

    (b) $\dfrac{\text{batteries}}{\text{cost}}$ $\dfrac{24}{\$12} = \dfrac{48}{b}$

    (c) $\dfrac{\text{Candy}}{\text{cost}}$ $\dfrac{25 \text{ pieces}}{\$5} = \dfrac{50 \text{ pieces}}{\$7.50}$

    Explain how you know this problem is a proportion problem.

    _____

    _____

3. Which is set up as a comparison of ratios problem?

    (a) $\dfrac{\text{Soft Drinks}}{\text{cost}}$ $\dfrac{20}{\$1} = \dfrac{10}{a}$

    (b) $\dfrac{\text{Highlighters}}{\text{cost}}$ $\dfrac{10}{\$5} = \dfrac{20}{\$10}$

    (c) $\dfrac{\text{inches}}{\text{miles}}$ $\dfrac{1}{x} = \dfrac{5}{500}$

    Explain how you know it is a comparison of ratios problem.

    _____

    _____

Unit 4

Name _____ Date _____

Activity 2

Solve the ratio problems. Show your work in the space provided.

1. You can buy gym socks this weekend at the big Athletic Trax store sale. Socks are three pairs for $10 or seven pairs for $30. Which is the better deal?

   _____

   _____

2. Your family stops at the gas station to fill up their tank with gas. The cost of a gallon of gas is $3.04 per gallon. About what will it cost for nine gallons of gas?

   _____

   _____

3. When you make lemonade, all you have to do is add eight ounces of syrup with 20 ounces of water. The bottle of lemonade syrup is 24 ounces. How much water would you need to add if you wanted to use the entire bottle of syrup?

   _____

   _____

4. The builders who are working to fix the bridge are mixing concrete. They mix the dry ingredients first, and then they add water. A mixture of concrete has sand, cement, and gravel. Here are the ingredients:

   1 pound cement

   2 pounds sand

   5 pounds gravel

   What is the percent of sand to the total mixture?

   _____

   What is the ratio of cement to gravel? _____

   If they want to use 10 pounds of sand for the mixture, how many pounds of cement do they need? _____

Name _____ Date _____

Activity 3

Solve the increasing and decreasing rate problems involving daylight. Make ratios from the word problems, then convert them to decimal numbers and percents. Show your work.

1. Jacksonville, Florida gets about 10 hours of daylight in February. It gets four more hours of daylight from February to May. Juneau, Alaska gets about six hours of daylight in December. It also gets four more hours of daylight from December to February.

    Is the percent of increase the same for both cities? _____

    In which city does the amount of daylight make a bigger difference? _____

    _____

    _____

2. Grand Rapids, Michigan loses five hours of daylight from June to November. It gets about 15 hours of daylight in June. Anchorage, Alaska loses about four hours of sunlight from October to December. It gets about 10 hours of daylight in October.

    Is the percent of decrease the same for both cities? _____

    In which city does losing daylight make a bigger difference? _____

    _____

    _____

mBook Reinforce Understanding
Use the mBook *Study Guide* to review lesson concepts.

Name _____ Date _____

 Skills Maintenance
Substituting Variables

Activity 1

Substitute the value for the variable and solve.

Model	Solve 35 + *m* if *m* = 5. ___40___

1. Solve 10 · *z* if *z* = 4 _____

2. Solve *x* – 15 if *x* = 39 _____

3. Solve 72 ÷ *n* if *n* = 8 _____

4. Solve *w* + 95 if *w* = 16 _____

5. Solve 6 · *m* if *m* = 7 _____

6. Solve *k* ÷ 4 if *k* = 112 _____

Name _____ Date _____

%÷ Apply Skills
Order of Operations

Activity 1

Evaluate the expressions using order of operations. Show your work.

Model	$3 + 6 \cdot 4 \div 8$ Evaluate	$3 + 6 \cdot 4 \div 8$ $3 + 24 \div 8$ $3 + 3 = 6$

1. $25 \div 5 \cdot 8 \div 4$

   Evaluate _____

   _____

   _____

2. $15 - 7 + 8 - 2$

   Evaluate _____

   _____

   _____

3. $5 + 4 \cdot 7 - 19$

   Evaluate _____

   _____

   _____

4. $26 - 9 + 6 \cdot 6 \div 4$

   Evaluate _____

   _____

   _____

Name _____ Date _____

 Problem-Solving Activity
3-D Shapes

Look at the two-dimensional shapes. Draw the shapes in three dimensions, then draw what they would look like if you unfolded them.

mBook Reinforce Understanding
Use the mBook *Study Guide* to review lesson concepts.

170 Unit 5 • Lesson 1

Name _____ Date _____

Skills Maintenance
Using Order of Operations

Activity 1

Evaluate the expressions using order of operations. Show your work.

1. $16 \div 4 \cdot 3 \div 6$

    Evaluate _____

    _____

    _____

2. $20 - 16 + 30 - 14$

    Evaluate _____

    _____

    _____

3. $5 + 7 \cdot 4 - 7$

    Evaluate _____

    _____

    _____

Unit 5

Name _____ Date _____

%÷ Apply Skills
Order of Operations: Parentheses

Activity 1

Use the rules for order of operations to evaluate the expressions.
Remember to solve all parentheses before any other operation.
Show your work.

1. $(4 + 3) \cdot (2 + 6)$

Evaluate _____

_____

_____

2. $25 \div (2 + 3) \cdot 9$

Evaluate _____

_____

_____

3. $2 \cdot (3 + 7) \div (10 - 6)$

Evaluate _____

_____

_____

4. $56 \div (8 - 1) \cdot (4 + 2)$

Evaluate _____

_____

_____

Name _____ Date _____

 Problem-Solving Activity
Sorting and Classifying Shapes

Select three shapes from each set and classify them based on a common attribute—something they all have in common. Be sure to use the letter label to identify the shapes you are comparing. Explain how the shapes you chose are alike.

1.

A   B   C   D   E

_____

_____

2.

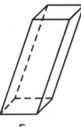   

F   G   H   I   J

_____

_____

mBook Reinforce Understanding
Use the mBook *Study Guide* to review lesson concepts.

Name _____ Date _____

Skills Maintenance
Using Order of Operations

Activity 1

Evaluate the expressions using order of operations. Show your work.

1. $3 \cdot (4 + 6) - 10$

    Evaluate _____

    _____

    _____

    _____

2. $(5 + 3) \cdot (4 - 1) \div 4$

    Evaluate _____

    _____

    _____

    _____

3. $5 + (14 - 6) \cdot 3 + (2 + 3)$

    Evaluate _____

    _____

    _____

    _____

4. $6 + 2 \cdot 3 + 4 + (27 - 19)$

    Evaluate _____

    _____

    _____

    _____

Name _____ Date _____

 Apply Skills
Putting PEMDAS in the Toolbox

Activity 1

Circle the part of the expression that you should evaluate first.

Model	$5 + 7 \cdot (3^2) + 8 - 4$

1. $8 + (2 + 7) - 15 \div 4$

2. $3 + 12 - 8 \div 2 \cdot 1$

3. $6 \cdot (4 + 3) - 4^2 \div 8$

4. $(5^2 - 8) + 7 \cdot 2$

Activity 2

Evaluate each expression using PEMDAS. Show your work.

1. $3^2 - (4 + 3) \cdot 8 - 4$

   Evaluate _____

   _____

   _____

   _____

2. $(27 - 11) + 28 \div 2^2 \cdot 3$

   Evaluate _____

   _____

   _____

   _____

3. $6 \cdot (12 - 4) - 12 - (3 \cdot 4)$

   Evaluate _____

   _____

   _____

   _____

Name _____ Date _____

Problem-Solving Activity
Identifying Ways Shapes Are Different

In each problem, you are given an attribute of a three-dimensional shape.
Sketch a picture of a shape that has this attribute. You don't need to use
any measurement tools. Next, sketch a picture of a shape that does not
have this attribute. Compare the two shapes you sketched, then explain
in writing how the attribute makes the shapes look different. Use as
many of the new vocabulary words discussed in Lesson 3 as you can.

1. Attribute: a vertex

    Sketch a shape with this attribute.

    Sketch a shape that does not have this attribute.

    Explain how this makes the shapes different.

    _____

    _____

    _____

2. Attribute: parallel bases

    Sketch a shape with this attribute.

    Sketch a shape that does not have this attribute.

    Explain how this makes the shapes different.

    _____

    _____

    _____

mBook Reinforce Understanding
Use the mBook *Study Guide* to review lesson concepts.

Name _____ Date _____

Skills Maintenance
Using Order of Operations

Activity 1

Evaluate the problems using PEMDAS. Show your work.

1. $3 \cdot (4 - 2^2) \cdot (8 + 2)$

    Evaluate _____

    _____

    _____

    _____

2. $(5 + 3) \cdot (7 - 5) + 3^2$

    Evaluate _____

    _____

    _____

    _____

Attributes of Shapes

Activity 2

For each shape, only one attribute applies. Circle that attribute.

1. (a) the shape has a square base

    (b) the shape has a vertex

    (c) the shape has a triangular base

2. (a) the shape has a square base

    (b) the shape has a vertex

    (c) the shape has a circular base

Unit 5

Name _____ Date _____

Apply Skills
Adding and Subtracting Integers

Activity 1

Tell the absolute value of each number.

1. $|-3|$ _____   **2.** $|3|$ _____

3. $|10|$ _____   **4.** $|-10|$ _____

Activity 2

Add or subtract the integers. Draw a modified number line to help you.

1. $5 - -3$ _____

2. $-3 + -2$ _____

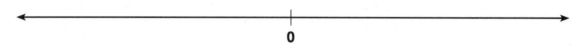

3. $22 - 42$ _____

4. $-12 - -11$ _____

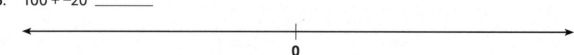

5. $-200 + 500$ _____

6. $100 + -20$ _____

mBook **Reinforce Understanding**
Use the mBook *Study Guide* to review lesson concepts.

Name _____ Date _____

Skills Maintenance
Order of Operations Using Integers

Activity 1

Evaluate the expressions. Remember the PEMDAS rules and the rules for working with integers. Show your work.

1. $-4 + -5 + (3 + -2)$

    Evaluate _____

    _____

    _____

    _____

2. $5^2 - 24 + -5$

    Evaluate _____

    _____

    _____

    _____

3. $6 \cdot (3 + 4) + -40 - -2$

    Evaluate _____

    _____

    _____

    _____

4. $-7 - -3 + 2^2 + (-2 - -3)$

    Evaluate _____

    _____

    _____

    _____

Name _____ Date _____

Problem-Solving Activity
Surface Area

Identify the two-dimensional shapes and formulas you need to find the surface area of each three-dimensional shape.

Model	What are the two-dimensional shapes that make up this shape? What formulas do you need to find its surface area?

Shape	Area Formula
Square	$A = b \cdot h$
Rectangle	$A = b \cdot h$

1. What are the two-dimensional shapes that make up this shape? Write the area formulas for these shapes.

Shape	Area Formula

2. What are the two-dimensional shapes that make up this shape? Write the area formulas for these shapes.

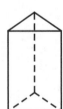

Shape	Area Formula

Name _____ Date _____

Problem-Solving Activity
Surface Area

Find the surface area of these shapes given their dimensions.

1. What is the surface area of the cube? _____

2. What is the surface area of the triangular prism? _____

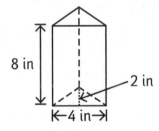

mBook Reinforce Understanding
Use the mBook *Study Guide* to review lesson concepts.

Unit 5 • Lesson 5   **181**

Name _____ Date _____

 ## Skills Maintenance
Variables and Substitution

> **Activity 1**

Substitute the value for the variable in each of the expressions and evaluate the expression. Show your work.

1. Evaluate $a + a + a$ for $a = 3$ _____

2. Evaluate $3 \cdot a$ for $a = 3$ _____

3. Evaluate $m + m$ for $m = 7$ _____

4. Evaluate $2 \cdot m$ for $m = 7$ _____

5. Evaluate $n + n + n + n$ for $n = 2$ _____

6. Evaluate $4 \cdot n$ for $n = 2$ _____

Name _____ Date _____

 ### Apply Skills
Algebraic Expressions and Special Symbols

Activity 1

Tell what expression is represented by each of the special symbols.
Remember that dark symbols are positive and light symbols are negative.

Model	Expression ___x + −2___

1. ▼ + ◻◻◻◻

   Expression _____

2. ▼ ▼ + ◻

   Expression _____

3. ▽ ▽ + ■■

   Expression _____

4. ▼ + ■■

   Expression _____

5. ▽ + ◻◻◻

   Expression _____

Name _____ Date _____

Activity 2

Write an expression with a variable that represents each word problem.
Circle the coefficient in the expression.

1. Hector makes twice as much as Cynthia. If Cynthia makes *m*
    dollars per week, how much does Hector make?

    _____

2. Tami is reading a road map. She notices the map has a key at the
    bottom that says 1 in = 50 miles. If Tami's trip measures *x* inches
    on the map, how many miles is that?

    _____

3. Suppose you are trying to explain to someone what it means to
    triple a recipe and the recipe calls for *b* cups of flour. How many
    cups of flour would you need for the recipe when you triple it?

    _____

4. There were 10 times as many students in Sam's middle school than
    at Kara's school. If there are *d* students in Kara's school, how many
    are in Sam's school?

    _____

---

mBook **Reinforce Understanding**
Use the mBook *Study Guide* to review lesson concepts.

Name _____ Date _____

 Skills Maintenance
Variable and Number Terms

Activity 1

Select the special symbols that match the expressions.

1. $x + 2$

    (a) ▽ + ◼

    (b) ▼ + ◻◻

    (c) ▼ + ◼◼

2. $-2x + 1$

    (a) ▽ ▽ + ◼

    (b) ▼ ▼ + ◻

    (c) ▼ + ◻◻

3. $2x + 3$

    (a) ▽ ▽ ▽ + ◼◼

    (b) ▼ ▼ ▼ + ◼◼

    (c) ▼ ▼ + ◼◼◼

4. $-x + -2$

    (a) ▽ + ◼◼

    (b) ▽ + ◻◻

    (c) ▽ ▽ + ◻

Name _____ Date _____

%÷ Apply Skills
≷x Simplifying Expressions by Combining Like Terms

Activity 1

Simplify the expressions by combining like terms. Use the special symbols to help you.

Model	$x + x + 2 + 3$  $2x + 5$

1. $x + 2x + 3 + 1$ _____

   _____

2. $4 + 2 + 2x + 2x$ _____

   _____

3. $2x + 2x + 1 + 1$ _____

   _____

4. $4 + 2 + 3x + 2x$ _____

   _____

Name _____ Date _____

Problem-Solving Activity
Surface Area of Pyramids

Find the surface area formula for a square pyramid. The base is a 4 × 4 square. The slant height of each face of the pyramid is 8 centimeters. Use your knowledge of area formulas to find the surface area of this shape. Explain how you found your answer when you are done.

Square Pyramid

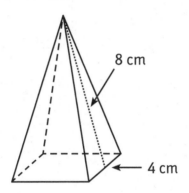

8 cm

4 cm

_____

_____

_____

_____

_____

 mBook Reinforce Understanding
Use the mBook *Study Guide* to review lesson concepts.

Name _____ Date _____

Skills Maintenance
Simplifying Expressions

Activity 1

Simplify the expressions by combining like terms. Show your work.

Model	$x + 2x + 3 + 2$ Answer $\underline{3x + 5}$

1. $2x + 3x + 7 + 1$ _____

_____

2. $8 + 2 + 2x + x$ _____

_____

3. $x + 2x + x + 5 + 7$ _____

_____

4. $12 + 10 + 8 + 3x$ _____

_____

5. $4x + 3x + 22$ _____

_____

6. $6 + 2 + 3 + 4 + 15x$ _____

_____

Name _____ Date _____

%÷ Apply Skills
<=x Adding Properties to the Toolbox

Activity 1

Simplify the expressions using special symbols. Use properties to move and group like terms. Use the property of opposites to cancel out terms.

Model

$2x + 3 + {-2} + {-x}$

Answer $x + 1$

1. $3a + {-2} + {-2a} + {-1}$ _____

2. $-5 + {-z} + 2z + 5$ _____

3. $-w + 2 + {-2w} + {-3}$ _____

4. $y + y + {-3} + {-2y} + {-2}$ _____

5. $-2b + {-b} + 2 + 1 + {-4} + 2b$ _____

Unit 5

Name _____ Date _____

 ### Problem-Solving Activity
Polyhedrons

Construct a polyhedron that is made out of a cube and six pyramids. Each pyramid will have four faces. The base is a square and the other three faces are triangles. Here are two views of the shape you will construct.

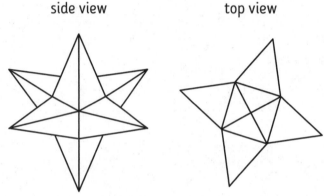

side view   top view

If you look carefully, you can see that the shape is made up of six pyramids, each with four faces, and a cube at the center.

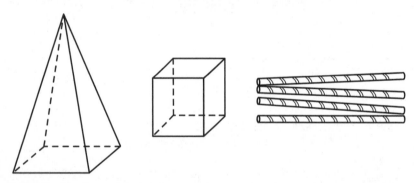

You can make your polyhedron out of plastic straws and tape. We are using straws that are about 10 inches, or 16 centimeters, long. The best straws to use are the ones that bend near the top. Look closely at the figures shown above. Look for a pattern to figure out how to construct the polyhedron.

Once you have a strategy, start to assemble the polyhedron one part at a time. You can cut each straw at the top to the point where it bends. Then push the cut part of the straw into another straw as shown on the next page. Then use tape to put sections of straw together.

Name _____ Date _____

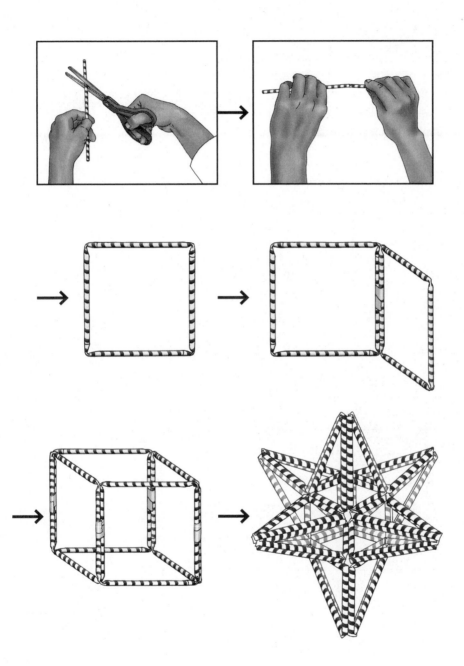

mBook Reinforce Understanding
Use the mBook *Study Guide* to review lesson concepts.

Name _____ Date _____

 Skills Maintenance
Simplifying Expressions

Activity 1

Combine like terms and simplify each expression.

1. $3x + x + 2 + -4$ _____

_____

_____

2. $x + -1 + 2 + 2x$ _____

_____

_____

3. $-x + 4 + 3x + -5$ _____

_____

_____

4. $2 + 3x + -3 + -1 + -2x$ _____

_____

_____

Name _____ Date _____

✎ Problem-Solving Activity
Polyhedrons and Surface Area

Find the two-dimensional shapes that make up each polyhedron.
Select the area formula from the list that matches each of the shapes
you identify.

Formulas: $A = b \cdot h$ $A = \pi r^2$ $A = \frac{1}{2} (b \cdot h)$

1.

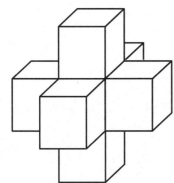

What 3-dimensional shape(s) make up this polyhedron?

_____

What 2-dimensional shape(s) make up this polyhedron?

_____

What area formula(s) will you use?

_____

2.

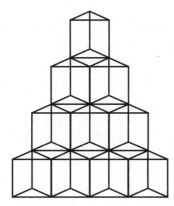

What 3-dimensional shape(s) make up this polyhedron?

_____

What 2-dimensional shape(s) make up this polyhedron?

_____

What area formula(s) will you use?

_____

3.

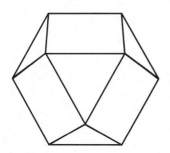

What 3-dimensional shape(s) make up this polyhedron?

_____

What 2-dimensional shape(s) make up this polyhedron?

_____

What area formula(s) will you use?

_____

Name _____ Date _____

Problem-Solving Activity
Polyhedrons and Surface Area

Compute the surface area of the polyhedron you constructed in the previous lesson. Use your metric ruler. Use the questions as a guide for organizing your work.

1. What shape(s) make up the faces of the polyhedron?

   _____

2. How many are there?

   _____

3. What are the dimensions of the shape? How do you find the area of that shape using these dimensions?

   _____

4. How do you put this information all together to find the surface area of the polyhedron?

   _____

   _____

   _____

   _____

   _____

5. In your own words, describe how you computed the surface area of the polyhedron.

   _____

   _____

   _____

   _____

   _____

mBook Reinforce Understanding
Use the mBook *Study Guide* to review lesson concepts.

Name _____ Date _____

Skills Maintenance
Special Symbols

Activity 1

Draw Vs and Ns to represent each expression. Use a red pen or pencil for negatives and a black pen or pencil for positives.

1. $x + {-2}$

_____

2. $-x + 3$

_____

3. $3x + 2$

_____

4. $-2x + {-1}$

_____

5. $x + {-3}$

_____

6. $3 + {-5}x + {-4}$

_____

Name _____ Date _____

Unit Review
Algebraic Rules and Properties

Activity 1

Evaluate the expressions using PEMDAS.

1. $3^2 + (5 \cdot 2) + 4$ _____

2. $20 \div 2 - 5$ _____

3. $9 \div 9 \cdot 7$ _____

4. $(10 + 8) \div (4 \div 2)$ _____

Activity 2

Solve the addition and subtraction problems.

1. $18 + -7$ _____   2. $-5 + 20$ _____

3. $-8 + -3$ _____   4. $-9 - -4$ _____

Name _____ Date _____

Activity 3

Write an expression for each word problem.

1. Gary's dog weighs three times as much as Lani's dog. If Lani's dog weighs *h* pounds, how much does Gary's dog weigh?

   _____

2. Harold's chocolate cake contains 4 times as much flour as it does sugar. If the cake has *r* amount of sugar, how much flour does it have?

   _____

3. There are 6 times as many people who watch basketball games than there are people who watch bowling on TV. If *v* is the number of people who watch bowling, how many people watch basketball?

   _____

Activity 4

Combine like terms and simplify the expressions.

1. $2a + 6 + 3a - 5$ _____

2. $5 + 3a - 4 - 2a$ _____

3. $-5 + 3a + 7 + 2 + 6a$ _____

4. $6a + 7 + -3 - 4a$ _____

5. $12a - 3a + 6 - 2a$ _____

Name _____ Date _____

Unit Review
Surface Area of Three-Dimensional Shapes

Activity 1

Find the surface area of each shape. Use the list of formulas to help you. You may use a calculator.

Remember that π = 3.14

Area of a circle = πr^2

Circumference of a circle = $2\pi r$

Area of a triangle = $\frac{1}{2} \cdot b \cdot h$

Area of a rectangle = $b \cdot h$

Area of a parallelogram = $b \cdot h$

1.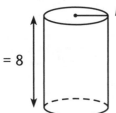

   $r = 2$

   $h = 8$

   Surface area _____

   _____

   _____

   _____

2.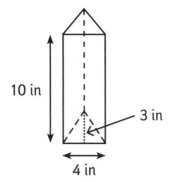

   10 in

   3 in

   4 in

   Surface area _____

   _____

   _____

   _____

Name _____ Date _____

3.

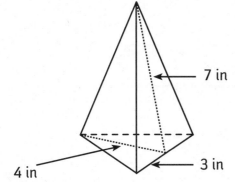

Surface area _____

_____

7 in

_____

4 in   3 in

_____

Activity 2

Find the surface area of the polyhedron.

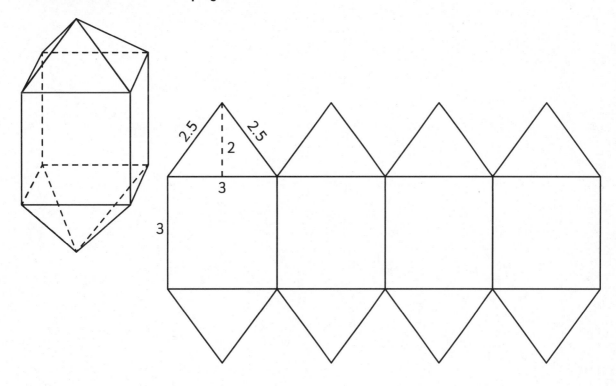

2.5   2.5

2

3

3

3

Surface area _____

Unit 5

Name _____ Date _____

 Skills Maintenance
Integer Addition and Subtraction

Activity 1

Solve the problems involving addition and subtraction of integers.

1. $-10 + 20$ _____

2. $15 - -5$ _____

3. $-3 - 5$ _____

4. $-25 + -35$ _____

5. $14 + -3$ _____

6. $-20 - -10$ _____

7. $15 + -5$ _____

8. $-3 + -5$ _____

Name _____ Date _____

%÷ Apply Skills
<x Multiplication and Division of Integers

Activity 1

Solve the problems involving multiplication and division of integers. Remember the PASS rules.

1. $-9 \cdot -5 =$ _____

2. $45 \div -9 =$ _____

3. $-7 \cdot$ _____ $= 56$

4. $-45 \div$ _____ $= -9$

5. $-56 \div 8 =$ _____

6. $-7 \cdot$ _____ $= 56$

7. $-81 \div$ _____ $= 9$

8. _____ $\cdot -4 = -28$

Activity 2

Solve the problems involving a mix of integer operations. Remember all of the integer rules.

1. $-3 + 7 =$ _____

2. $17 - -2 =$ _____

3. $-6 \cdot -6 =$ _____

4. $28 \div -4 =$ _____

5. $-6 \cdot$ _____ $= 42$

6. $-32 \div$ _____ $= 4$

7. $-12 - 15 =$ _____

8. $18 - 25 =$ _____

Name _____ Date _____

Problem-Solving Activity
Concept of Volume

Estimate the volume of common three-dimensional objects, such as pans
or boxes, using informal measuring tools like the materials shown in the
Student Text.

On your paper, write the name of the object you are measuring and its
shape. Then fill the object with one of the materials from the *Student
Text* and estimate the volume by describing how much of the material
you need to fill it. Write the estimate on your paper next to the object. Be
sure to include the units (e.g., 2 cups of water, 10 marbles, 15 cubes, or 1
$\frac{1}{2}$ cups of rice). Make a table that looks like this on your paper and fill in
your findings.

Object	Shape	Unit of Measure	Volume Estimate
Pan	Cylinder	Water	About 3 cups of water
Box	Rectangular prism	Rice	About 5 cups of rice

After you measure all the objects, compare your volume estimates for
the various three-dimensional objects with other students sitting around
you. Are your answers the same? Explain why or why not. How do you
think your estimates compare to an exact measurements? How are the
units the same? How are they different?

_____

_____

_____

_____

_____

_____

_____

_____

mBook Reinforce Understanding
Use the mBook *Study Guide* to review lesson concepts.

Name _____ Date _____

Skills Maintenance
Evaluating Expressions With Integers

Activity 1

Evaluate the expressions using **PEMDAS** rules and **PASS** rules.
Show your work.

1. $25 - (3 - -2) + 2 \cdot -3$ _____

2. $4^2 \div (-2 + -2) - (8 \cdot -1)$ _____

3. $(-5 - 7) + (-2 \cdot -4) - -15$ _____

4. $6^2 - (-4 \cdot -8) + 2 - -2$ _____

Name _____ Date _____

Problem-Solving Activity
Measuring Volume and Cubic Units

Use the formula Volume = height · width · depth to find the volume of the cubes and rectangular prisms.

1. The cube's volume is _____.

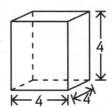

2. The rectangular prism's volume is _____.

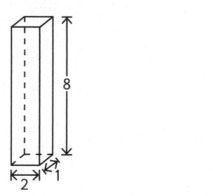

3. The rectangular prism's volume is _____.

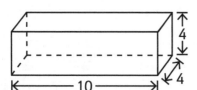

4. The cube's volume is _____.

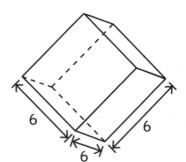

Name _____ Date _____

Problem-Solving Activity
Measuring Volume and Cubic Units

Use a cubic unit—a sugar cube—to compute the volume of a box. The sugar cube makes a good tool for measuring volume accurately since it is a unit of measure that fits neatly in the box without a lot of gaps. Once you fill the bottom of the box, record the number of sugar cubes you used. Then begin the second layer of sugar cubes, and continue until the box is filled. Record the number of layers it took to fill the box. What is the volume of the box? Is this an estimate or an exact measurement? Explain your answer.

_____

_____

_____

_____

_____

mBook Reinforce Understanding
Use the mBook *Study Guide* to review lesson concepts.

Name _____ Date _____

 Skills Maintenance
Substitution

Activity 1

Substitute the value for the variable in each of the expressions, then solve the problems.

Model	Evaluate $3m$ if $m = -2$. $3 \cdot -2 = -6$

1. Evaluate $4x$ if $x = 10$. _____

2. Evaluate $-2 - w$ if $w = -5$. _____

3. Evaluate $-3a$ if $a = -2$. _____

4. Evaluate $4 - h$ if $h = -5$. _____

5. Evaluate $n \div -5$ if $n = -45$. _____

Name _____ Date _____

%÷ Apply Skills
Substitution and Evaluating Algebraic Expressions

Activity 1

Evaluate each of the expressions using two methods.

In Method 1, simplify and then substitute. In Method 2, substitute and then simplify.

1. Evaluate $3x + 7 + 2x + 10$ for $x = -2$.

    Method 1: Simplify and then substitute.

    Answer _____

    Method 2: Substitute and then simplify.

    Answer _____

2. Evaluate $-4 - x - -3 + 2x$ for $x = 1$.

    Method 1: Simplify and then substitute.

    Answer _____

    Method 2: Substitute and then simplify.

    Answer _____

3. Evaluate $-x + 2x - 5 \cdot -3 + -x$ for $x = -1$.

    Method 1: Simplify and then substitute.

    Answer _____

    Method 2: Substitute and then simplify.

    Answer _____

Name _____ Date _____

 Problem-Solving Activity
Bases and the Volume of Prisms

Use the paper models on the next page to find the area of three different prisms. When you put the prisms together, they should look like this:

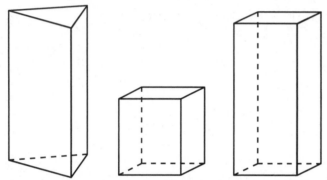

Use a metric ruler to measure the base and height of each prism. Measure the dimensions to the closest centimeter and round your measurement, if necessary. Remember to use these basic formulas for the base:

Area of a triangle = $\frac{1}{2} \cdot b \cdot h$

Area of a square or rectangle = $b \cdot h$

	Triangular Prism	Cube	Rectangular Prism
Base			
Height			
Volume			

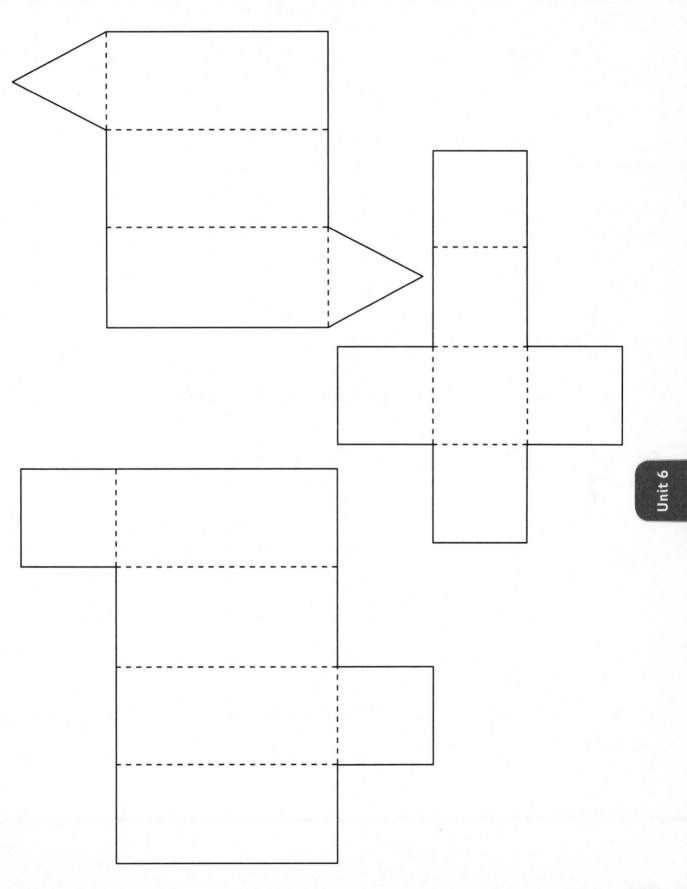

This page intentionally left blank.

Name _____ Date _____

⚙ Skills Maintenance
Number Patterns with Consecutive Numbers

Activity 1

Fill in the consecutive numbers that come before and after each of the integers. Sketch a modified number line if it helps.

Model	_____ −13 _____ , −12, _____ −11 _____

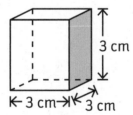

1. _____ , 0, _____

2. _____ , _____ , 4

3. 111, _____ , 113

4. _____ , −1, _____

Volume of Common Prisms

Activity 2

Find the volume of each shape. You are given the Base and the height.

1.

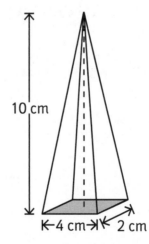

3 cm

⊢ 3 cm →⊬ 3 cm

If the Base is 9 cm², what is the volume of the cube? _____

2.

10 cm

⊢ 4 cm →⊬ 2 cm

If the Base is 8 cm², what is the volume of the triangular prism? _____

Name _____ Date _____

 ## Apply Skills
Writing and Evaluating Expressions

Activity 1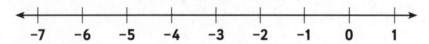

Test the general pattern for consecutive numbers represented by the expressions x, $x + 1$, and $x + 2$ by selecting three consecutive numbers from the number line. Make the first number x.

$$\xleftarrow{\hspace{1cm}} \quad -7 \quad -6 \quad -5 \quad -4 \quad -3 \quad -2 \quad -1 \quad 0 \quad 1 \xrightarrow{\hspace{1cm}}$$

1. Select three consecutive numbers from the number line.

   What are your three consecutive numbers?

   _____ , _____ , _____

   Prove that the general pattern x, $x + 1$, and $x + 2$ is true for these three numbers.

   $x =$ _____ $x + 1 =$ _____ $x + 2 =$ _____

2. Select a different set of three consecutive numbers from the number line.

   What are your three consecutive numbers?

   _____ , _____ , _____

   Prove that the general pattern x, $x + 1$, and $x + 2$ is true for these three numbers.

   $x =$ _____ $x + 1 =$ _____ $x + 2 =$ _____

Name _____ Date _____

Test the general pattern for consecutive numbers represented by the expressions x, $x + 1$, and $x + 2$ by selecting three consecutive numbers from the number grid. Make the first number x.

1	2	3	4	5	6	7	8	9	10
11	12	13	14	15	16	17	18	19	20
21	22	23	24	25	26	27	28	29	30
31	32	33	34	35	36	37	38	39	40
41	42	43	44	45	46	47	48	49	50

1. Select three consecutive numbers from the number grid.

   What are your three consecutive numbers?

   _____ , _____ , _____

   Prove that the general pattern x, $x + 1$, and $x + 2$ is true for the three numbers you selected.

   $x =$ _____ $x + 1 =$ _____ $x + 2 =$ _____

2. Select a different set of three consecutive numbers from the number grid.

   What are your three consecutive numbers?

   _____ , _____ , _____

   Prove that the general pattern x, $x + 1$, and $x + 2$ is true for these three numbers.

   $x =$ _____ $x + 1 =$ _____ $x + 2 =$ _____

Name _____ Date _____

Select three shaded numbers from the grid. Write three different sets of expressions for these numbers.

1.

1	2	3	4	5	6	7	8	9	10
11	12	13	14	15	16	17	18	19	20
21	22	23	24	25	26	27	28	29	30
31	32	33	34	35	36	37	38	39	40
41	42	43	44	45	46	47	48	49	50
51	52	53	54	55	56	57	58	59	60
61	62	63	64	65	66	67	68	69	70
71	72	73	74	75	76	77	78	79	80
81	82	83	84	85	86	87	88	89	90
91	92	93	94	95	96	97	98	99	100

_____

_____

_____

2.

1	2	3	4	5	6	7	8	9	10
11	12	13	14	15	16	17	18	19	20
21	22	23	24	25	26	27	28	29	30
31	32	33	34	35	36	37	38	39	40
41	42	43	44	45	46	47	48	49	50
51	52	53	54	55	56	57	58	59	60
61	62	63	64	65	66	67	68	69	70
71	72	73	74	75	76	77	78	79	80
81	82	83	84	85	86	87	88	89	90
91	92	93	94	95	96	97	98	99	100

_____

_____

_____

mBook **Reinforce Understanding**
Use the mBook *Study Guide* to review lesson concepts.

Name _____ Date _____

 Skills Maintenance
Writing Different Expressions to Describe a Pattern

Activity 1

Write two different expressions to describe the three consecutive numbers in each problem.

Model	70, 75, 80
	Answer If $x = 70$, the pattern is x, $x + 5$, $x + 10$.
	If $x = 75$, the pattern is $x - 5$, x, $x + 5$.

1. 1, 2, 3

2. 2, 4, 6

Calculating Volume

Activity 2

Compute the volume for each of the objects.

1.

If a cube has a Base of 25 cm^2 and a height of 5, what is its volume? _____

2.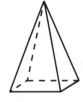

If a triangular prism has a Base of 10 cm^2 and a height of 6, what is its volume? _____

Name _____ Date _____

Apply Skills
Commonsense Algebraic Properties

Activity 1

Write a general statement that describes the commonsense property shown by the examples in each problem. Then write the name of that property.

Model	$5 + 0 = 5 \qquad 2.5 + 0 = 2.5 \qquad \frac{1}{2} + 0 = \frac{1}{2}$
	General Statement _____$n + 0 = n$_____
	Name of Property ___Additive Identity Property___

1. $6 \cdot 1 = 6 \qquad \frac{1}{4} \cdot 1 = \frac{1}{4} \qquad 37.5 \cdot 1 = 37.5$

   General Statement _____

   Name of Property _____

2. $3 \cdot 0 = 0 \qquad \frac{4}{5} \cdot 0 = 0 \qquad 100.12 \cdot 0 = 0$

   General Statement _____

   Name of Property _____

3. $2 \cdot \frac{1}{2} = 1 \qquad 5 \cdot \frac{1}{5} = 1 \qquad 75 \cdot \frac{1}{75} = 1$

   General Statement _____

   Name of Property _____

4. $3 + -3 = 0 \qquad \frac{2}{3} + -\frac{2}{3} = 0 \qquad 1.25 + -1.25 = 0$

   General Statement _____

   Name of Property _____

5. $\frac{2}{3} \cdot \frac{3}{2} = 1 \qquad \frac{4}{5} \cdot \frac{5}{4} = 1 \qquad \frac{100}{200} \cdot \frac{200}{100} = 1$

   General Statement _____

   Name of Property _____

mBook **Reinforce Understanding**

Use the mBook *Study Guide* to review lesson concepts.

Name _____ Date _____

Skills Maintenance
Commonsense Properties

Activity 1

Give three examples for each of the commonsense properties below. A general pattern is written with variables.

Model	Multiplicative Identity Property, $n \cdot 1 = n$ $3 \cdot 1 = 3$ $50 \cdot 1 = 50$ $100 \cdot 1 = 100$

1. Additive Inverse Property, $n + -n = 0$

   _____

   _____

   _____

2. Multiplicative Property of 0, $n \cdot 0 = 0$

   _____

   _____

3. Multiplicative Inverse Property, $n \cdot \dfrac{1}{n} = 1$

   _____

   _____

Unit 6

Name _____ Date _____

 Problem-Solving Activity
The Volume of Cones and Pyramids

For each of the shapes, sketch what the shape would look like if you stacked its base. Then draw lines on your sketch to show an approximation of how their volumes differ.

1. **Cone**   **Sketch of Stacked Bases**

2. **Rectangular Pyramid**   **Sketch of Stacked Bases**

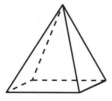

3. **Triangular Pyramid**   **Sketch of Stacked Bases**

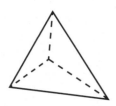

Name _____ Date _____

 Problem-Solving Activity
The Volume of Cones and Pyramids

Find the volume of the prism or cylinder and the shape inside, then compare them.

1. The height of the pyramid and the prism is the same. The Base for each object is also the same.

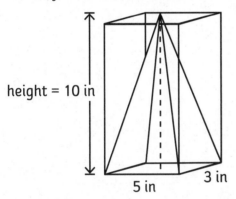

height = 10 in

5 in   3 in

(a) What is the volume of the prism? _____

(b) What is the volume of the pyramid? _____

2.   height = 15

radius = 5

(a) What is the volume of the cylinder? _____

(b) What is the volume of the cone? _____

Name _____ Date _____

3.

The volume of this cylinder is 300 in³.

What is the volume of a cone with the same height and Base? _____

4.

The volume of this pyramid is 150 in³.

What is the volume of a prism with the same height and Base? _____

mBook Reinforce Understanding
Use the mBook *Study Guide* to review lesson concepts.

Name _____ Date _____

Skills Maintenance
Commonsense Properties

Activity 1

Give three examples of each of the properties.

Model	Give three examples of the Commutative Property for Addition. General Statement $a + b = b + a$ $3 + 1 = 1 + 3$ $\quad \frac{1}{3} + \frac{2}{3} = \frac{2}{3} + \frac{1}{3}$ $\quad 2.75 + 0.25 = 0.25 + 2.75$

1. Give three examples of the Additive Inverse Property.

   General Statement: $n + -n = 0$

   _____

   _____

   _____

2. Give three examples of the Associative Property for Multiplication.

   General Statement: $a \cdot (b \cdot c) = (a \cdot b) \cdot c$

   _____

   _____

   _____

Finding the Volume

Activity 2

Find the volume of the cone and pyramid.

1. This cone has a Base of 10 cm² and a height of 7 cm.

   Volume = $\frac{1}{3}$ Base · height

   What is the cone's volume? _____

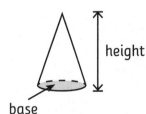

2. This pyramid has a Base of 5 cm² and a height of 8 cm.

   Volume = $\frac{1}{3}$ Base · height

   What is the pyramid's volume? _____

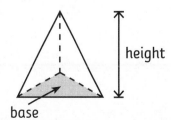

Name _____ Date _____

Apply Skills
Distributive Property

Activity 1

Use the distributive property to simplify the expressions. Show all of your work.

1. $3(x + 2)$

2. $4(2w - 1)$

3. $a(a + 2)$

4. $8(3 - z)$

5. $4(2 + b)$

6. $-2(c - 4)$

Name _____ Date _____

Activity 2

Read each statement carefully, then translate it into an expression. Do not simplify it. Use *h* as the variable in the expression. Here is a hint, there are only three problems where you will have an expression with a coefficient and parentheses.

1. A number minus 7 _____

2. 4 times a number plus 5 _____

3. $\frac{1}{2}$ of a number _____

4. 2 times the sum of a number plus 3 _____

5. 7 times a number minus 7 _____

6. 5 times the sum of a number plus 1 _____

7. A number times a number _____

8. 3 times a number minus 2 _____

9. 3 times the sum of a number plus −4 _____

10. A number plus $\frac{3}{4}$ _____

mBook **Reinforce Understanding**
Use the **mBook** *Study Guide* to review lesson concepts.

Unit 6 • Lesson 7 **223**

Unit 6

Name _____ Date _____

 Skills Maintenance
Distributive Property

Activity 1

Use the distributive property to simplify each problem.

1. $5(a + 2)$ _____

2. $-2(b + 5)$ _____

3. $2(2 + c)$ _____

4. $d(d + 2)$ _____

5. $2(m - 4)$ _____

6. $-5(2 - n)$ _____

Name _____ Date _____

 Problem-Solving Activity

The Volume of Spheres

Find the volume of each sphere using this formula: $V = \frac{4}{3}\pi r^3$. Use 3.14 to estimate pi. Show your work.

1.

$r = 2$

Show your work here.

2.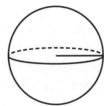

$r = 4$

Show your work here.

The volume is _____.

The volume is _____.

3.

$r = 1$

Show your work here.

4.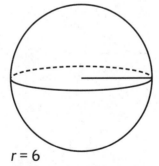

$r = 6$

Show your work here.

The volume is _____.

The volume is _____.

Name _____ Date _____

Problem-Solving Activity
The Volume of Spheres

The Sunland Packing Company packs fresh fruit that is shipped all over the United States. Sunland has a special way of packing a box of fruit. The drawing shows how the grapefruit is packed.

What is the volume of one grapefruit? What is the volume for all of the grapefruit? Figure out the dimensions of the box that holds all of the grapefruit. The box should be just big enough so the grapefruit cannot move. Finally, compare the volume of all the grapefruit to the volume for the box that will hold these grapefruit.

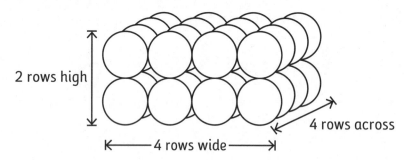

The radius of one grapefruit is 3 inches.

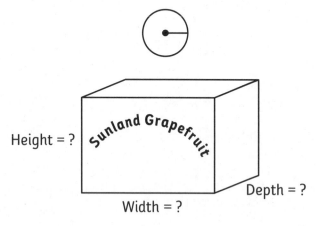

Volume of 1 grapefruit _____

Volume of all grapefruit _____

Dimensions of the box _____

Volume of the box _____

mBook Reinforce Understanding
Use the mBook *Study Guide* to review lesson concepts.

Name _____ Date _____

Skills Maintenance
Properties

Activity 1

Look at the general statement and tell what property is being demonstrated in each problem.

Model	$3(x + 4) = 3x + 12$ Distributive Property, $n(a + b) = na + nb$

1. $5 + 0 = 5$ _____

2. $5 \cdot 0 = 0$ _____

3. $5 + 6 = 6 + 5$ _____

4. $5 + -5 = 0$ _____

Unit 6

Name _____ Date _____

 Problem-Solving Activity
Finding the Volume of Complex Objects

Look at each of the shapes and select the correct volume formula for it. Then find the volume.

1. What is this shape's volume formula? (circle one)

    (a) $V = \text{Base} \cdot \text{height}$

    (b) $V = \frac{1}{3} \text{Base} \cdot \text{height}$

    (c) $V = \frac{4}{3}\pi r^3$

    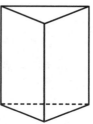

    Compute the volume of this shape if it has a Base of 4 cm² and a height of 10cm. _____

    Show your work here.

2. What is this shape's volume formula? (circle one)

    (a) $V = \text{Base} \cdot \text{height}$

    (b) $V = \frac{1}{3} \text{Base} \cdot \text{height}$

    (c) $V = \frac{4}{3}\pi r^3$

    Compute the volume of this shape if it has a Base of 2 cm² and a height of 6 cm. _____

    Show your work here.

Name _____ Date _____

3. What is this shape's volume formula? (circle one)

    (a) $V = $ Base $\cdot$ height

    (b) $V = \frac{1}{3}$ Base $\cdot$ height

    (c) $V = \frac{4}{3}\pi r^3$

    Compute the volume of this shape if it has a Base of 8 cm² and a height of 7 cm. _____

    Show your work here.

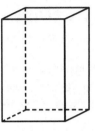

4. What is this shape's volume formula? (circle one)

    (a) $V = $ Base $\cdot$ height

    (b) $V = \frac{1}{3}$ Base $\cdot$ height

    (c) $V = \frac{4}{3}\pi r^3$

    Compute the volume of this shape if it has a Base of 4 cm² and a height of 11 cm. _____

    Show your work here.

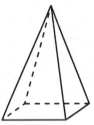

Unit 6

Name _____ Date _____

Problem-Solving Activity
Finding the Volume of Complex Objects

Sketch a picture of a polyhedron that uses two or more of the shapes from Questions 1–4. Find the volume of the polyhedron using the dimensions and measurements you know.

Sketch your compound shape here.

Find your shape's volume. Make sure to look for a pattern when you determine the total volume. Think carefully about the parts of the polyhedron that you cannot see. Make sure that you can explain how you figured out the volume of the polyhedron. Be able to describe what strategies you used to find the volume.

What is its volume? _____

_____

_____

_____

_____

_____

_____

mBook Reinforce Understanding
Use the mBook *Study Guide* to review lesson concepts.

Name _____ Date _____

Skills Maintenance
Using Properties With Integers

Activity 1

Use the properties and rules you know to simplify the problems.

1. $3(m - 4) + 10 \div 2$

2. $15 \div -3 + 10(9 \div 3) \cdot 2x$

3. $4(4 + k) + k(k - 15)$

Name _____ Date _____

Unit Review
More Algebraic Rules and Properties

Activity 1

Use PEMDAS to evaluate these expressions with integers.

1. $-4 \cdot 3 \div (6 + -2)$

2. $-25 \div -5 + -3$

3. $(20 + 10) \div 2 \cdot -3$

4. $4^2 + -6 - -3$

5. $6 \cdot (-8 \div -4)$

Activity 2

Use substitution to evaluate the expressions. Remember the PASS rules.

1. Let $f = -2$ $3f + 6 - 5$

2. Let $m = 9$ $3m - -4$

3. Let $v = -1$ $4v + 10 + -6v$

4. Let $z = 10$ $-2z + 5$

5. Let $y = 5$ $3y - (2 \cdot 10)$

Name _____ Date _____

Activity 3

Use the distributive property to simplify these expressions.

1. $-2(v + 7)$ _____

2. $-3(b - 5)$ _____

3. $6(e + 6)$ _____

4. $2(-w + 10)$ _____

5. $5(g - 5)$ _____

Unit 6

Name _____ Date _____

Unit Review
Volume of Three-Dimensional Shapes

Activity 1

Use a calculator to find the volume of each shape. Use these important area formulas:

Area of a circle = πr^2 Volume of a prism = $B \cdot h$

Area of a triangle = $\frac{1}{2} \cdot b \cdot h$ Volume of a cylinder = $B \cdot h$

Area of a square or rectangle = $b \cdot h$ Volume of a pyramid = $\frac{1}{3} \cdot B \cdot h$

1.   What is the volume of this pyramid? _____

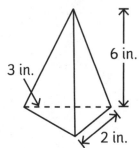

3 in.   6 in.   2 in.

2.   What is the volume of this cylinder? _____

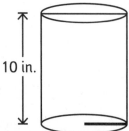

10 in.   radius = 3 in.

3.   What is the volume of this prism? _____

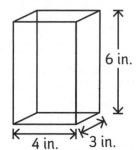

6 in.   4 in.   3 in.

mBook Reinforce Understanding
Use the mBook *Study Guide* to review lesson concepts.

Name _____ Date _____

 Skills Maintenance
Algebraic Expressions

Activity 1

Find the value of the variable that makes the statement true.

Model	If $x + 7 = 10$, what is the value of x? Answer _____x_____ = 3

1. If $72 \div y = 8$, what is the value of y?

   $y =$ _____

2. If $m \cdot 7 = 56$, what is the value of m?

   $m =$ _____

3. If $50 - n = 25$, what is the value of n?

   $n =$ _____

4. If $z + 212 = 300$, what is the value of z?

   $z =$ _____

Name _____ Date _____

 Apply Skills
Introduction to Algebraic Equations

Activity 1

Decide whether the two sides of each equation are equal by simplifying the expressions on either side.

Model	$27 - 14 + 8 \cdot 2 = 3^2 + 4^2 + 2^2$

Solving on the left

$27 - 14 + \mathbf{8 \cdot 2} = 3^2 + 4^2 + 2^2$

$\mathbf{27 - 14} + 16 = 3^2 + 4^2 + 2^2$

$\mathbf{13 + 16} = 3^2 + 4^2 + 2^2$

$29 = 3^2 + 4^2 + 2^2$

Solving on the right

$29 = \mathbf{3^2} + 4^2 + 2^2$

$29 = 9 + \mathbf{4^2} + 2^2$

$29 = 9 + 16 + \mathbf{2^2}$

$29 = 9 + 16 + 4$

$29 = \mathbf{9 + 16} + 4$

$29 = \mathbf{25 + 4}$

$29 = 29$

Both of the sides equal 29.

1. $54 - 30 + 40 = 8^2$

Show your work here.

Name _____ Date _____

2.

$$\frac{(8 + 7) \qquad = \qquad 40 + 35}{\triangle}$$

Show your work here.

3.

$$\frac{10^2 - 9^2 \qquad = \qquad 10 + 3^2}{\triangle}$$

Show your work here.

4.

$$\frac{25 \cdot 10 \qquad = \qquad 5 \cdot 2 \cdot 5 \cdot 2 \cdot 5^2}{\triangle}$$

Show your work here.

Name _____ Date _____

Problem-Solving Activity
Geometric Construction and Angle Measurement

Follow the instructions for each problem and make a set of perpendicular line segments and parallel lines. Explain your constructions and use as many of the geometric terms you learned as possible.

X •———————————————————————• Y

1. Using line segment XY, draw perpendicular lines with a ruler and compass.

   _____

   _____

   _____

   _____

2. Using line segment LM, draw a line that is parallel to the segment.

   X •———————————————————————————————————• Y

   _____

   _____

   _____

   _____

Name _____ Date _____

Skills Maintenance
Balanced Equations

Activity 1

Show that each equation is balanced by simplifying the equations on both sides of the equal sign.

1. $\dfrac{45 + 45 \qquad = \qquad 10 \cdot 3^2}{}$

   Show your work here.

2. $\dfrac{72 \div 8 + 6 \qquad = \qquad (2 + 3) \cdot 3}{}$

   Show your work here.

3. $\dfrac{102 - 77 \qquad = \qquad 3^2 + 4^2}{}$

   Show your work here.

Unit 7

Name _____ Date _____

Apply Skills
Balancing an Equation

Activity 1

Write an expression on the blank side of the scale that is equal to the other equation. Your expression should include one operation or more and more than one term. Then show that the two sides are balanced.

Model

$$4 + 5 \quad =$$

Begin by solving the left side, $4 + 5 = 9$.
Then think of a different expression for representing 9.
Example $9 = 109 - 100$.
Answer $4 + 5 = 109 - 100$

$$4 + 5 \quad = \quad 109 - 100$$

Prove the sides are equal by simplifying.
$4 + 5 = 9$ and $109 - 100 = 9$
$9 = 9$;   the equation is balanced.

1.

$$2^2 + 45 \quad =$$

(a) Simplify the left side. _____

(b) Think of a different expression for representing the same thing and write it above.

(c) Prove the equation is balanced by simplifying both sides. Show your work here.

2.

$$= \quad 5^2 + 6^2 - 11$$

(a) Simplify the right side. _____

(b) Think of a different expression for representing the same thing and write it above.

(c) Prove the equation is balanced by simplifying both sides. Show your work here.

3.

$$5(8 + 2) \quad =$$

(a) Simplify the left side. _____

(b) Think of a different expression for representing the same thing and write it above.

(c) Prove the equation is balanced by simplifying both sides. Show your work here.

4.

$$= \quad 900 \div (3 \cdot 10) + 6$$

(a) Simplify the right side. _____

(b) Think of a different expression for representing the same thing and write it above.

(c) Prove the equation is balanced by simplifying both sides. Show your work here.

Unit 7

Name _____ Date _____

Problem-Solving Activity
Bisecting Angles

Use what you learned about creating a perpendicular line. Then use a
ruler or straight edge and a compass to construct each angle.

1. An angle that measures 45°

2. An angle that measures 135°

3. An angle that measures 225°

4. An angle that measures 315°

mBook Reinforce Understanding
Use the mBook *Study Guide* to review lesson concepts.

Name _____ Date _____

 Skills Maintenance
Geometric Constructions

Select the term that describes the construction.

1.

   (a) parallel

   (b) perpendicular

   (c) bisector

2.

   (a) parallel

   (b) perpendicular

   (c) bisector

3.

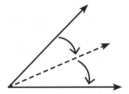

   (a) parallel

   (b) perpendicular

   (c) bisector

Name _____ Date _____

⊞ Apply Skills
Another Way to Think About Balancing Equations

Activity 1

Substitute equivalent shapes until both sides are exactly the same. Use these equivalences.

$$\triangle \triangle \triangle = \bigcirc$$

$$\square \square \square \square \square = \bigcirc$$

$$\square \square = \triangle$$

Model	Answer
	$\bigcirc \triangle = \triangle \triangle \triangle \square \square$
	$\bigcirc \triangle = \triangle \triangle \triangle \square \square$
	$\bigcirc \triangle \qquad \bigcirc \qquad \triangle$

1. $\bigcirc = \square \square \triangle \triangle$

2. $\square \square \bigcirc = \triangle \triangle \triangle \triangle$

3. $\triangle \triangle \triangle \triangle = \square \square \square \square \square \square \square$

Name _____ Date _____

Activity 2

Find the relative weight for each shape. Use information from both scales or cancel out shapes that are the same on the same scale to answer each problem. The weight of each of the shapes changes for each problem.

1. Find the weight of the square.

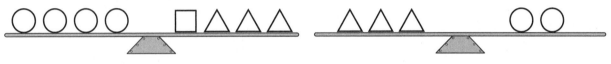

□ = _____

2. Find the weight of the circle.

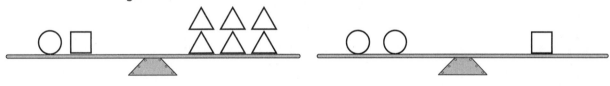

○ = _____

3. Find the weight of the square.

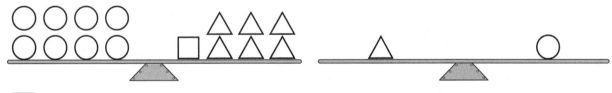

□ = _____

4. Find the weight of the square.

□ = _____

mBook **Reinforce Understanding**
Use the mBook *Study Guide* to review lesson concepts.

Unit 7 • Lesson 3   **245**

Name _____ Date _____

 ## Skills Maintenance
Balanced Scales

Activity 1

Use cancellation and the balance scales to find the value of a certain shape in each problem.

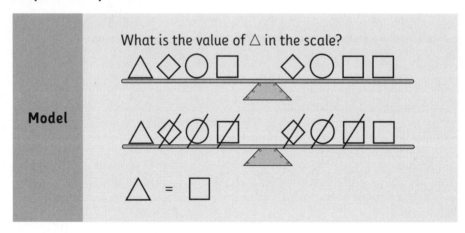

1. What is the value of △ in the scale?

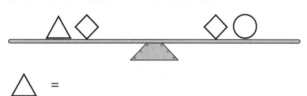

△ = _____

2. What is the value of ○ in the scale?

△◇   ◇○

○ = _____

3. What is the value of □ in the scale?

△◇○○□   △◇○□□

□ = _____

Name _____ Date _____

Apply Skills
Equations With Variables

Activity 1

Solve the equations using special symbols and properties. Check your answer by substituting the value of the variable into the original equation. Gray symbols represent negatives.

Model	$x + 3 = 5$ Represent the problem using special symbols: Add the inverse of 3 to each side to get the variable alone: Cancel inverses since they equal 0: Write the special symbols that are left: Write use variables and numbers: $x = 2$

1. $y - 5 = 4$ Show your work here:

   Check your answer here: _____

2. $z + 3 = -2$ Show your work here:

   Check your answer here: _____

Name _____ Date _____

Problem-Solving Activity
Determining Measurements of Angles

Use algebraic equations to find the missing angle measurements in each problem. Be sure to show all your work.

1. What is the measure of ∠b? _____

2. What is the measure of ∠r? _____

3. What is the measure of ∠c? _____

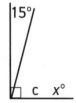

Name _____ Date _____

4. What is the measure of ∠v? _____

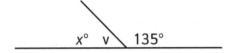

5. What is the measure of ∠j? _____

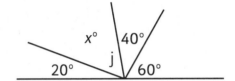

mBook **Reinforce Understanding**
Use the mBook *Study Guide* to review lesson concepts.

Unit 7 • Lesson 4   **249**

Name _____ Date _____

 Skills Maintenance
Solving Simple Equations

Activity 1

Use the rules and properties you learned to solve the algebraic equations.
Then check the answers by substituting the value of the variable into the
original equations.

1. $x - 2 = 4$

    Show your work here.

    Check your work here. _____

2. $3 + y = -1$

    Show your work here.

    Check your work here. _____

3. $z - -5 = -2$

    Show your work here.

    Check your work here. _____

Name _____ Date _____

 Apply Skills
Equations With Coefficients

> **Activity 1**

Use special symbols to solve the simple equations.

1. $3x = 18$ Show your work here.

    $x =$ _____   Check your work here: _____

2. $\frac{1}{2}y = 4$ Show your work here.

    $y =$ _____   Check your work here: _____

3. $6w = 54$ Show your work here.

    $w =$ _____   Check your work here: _____

4. $\frac{1}{5}a = 5$ Show your work here.

    $a =$ _____   Check your work here. _____

mBook **Reinforce Understanding**
Use the mBook *Study Guide* to review lesson concepts.

Name _____ Date _____

Skills Maintenance
Finding the Missing Angle

Activity 1

Make algebraic expressions to find the missing angle in each of the triangles. Remember the sum of the interior angles of a triangle is 180 degrees.

1.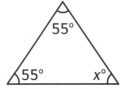

Write your equation here.

_____

Show your work here.

The missing angle, x, has a measurement of _____

2.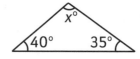

Write your equation here.

_____

Show your work here.

The missing angle, x, has a measurement of _____

Simple Equations

Activity 2

Find the missing number to complete the equations.

1. $\frac{1}{3} \cdot 3 =$ _____

2. $3 \cdot$ _____ $= 1$

3. _____ $\cdot \frac{1}{3} = 1$

4. $\frac{2}{3} \cdot \frac{3}{2} =$ _____

5. $\frac{3}{2} \cdot$ _____ $= 1$

6. _____ $\cdot \frac{2}{3} = 1$

Name _____ Date _____

 Apply Skills
More Equations With Coefficients

Activity 1

Set up each problem as a proportion. Then use the cross-multiplying strategy to solve the problems. Be sure to show all of your work.

1. Johnson's Furniture Store gets deliveries of new sofas every month. The delivery truck carries 10 sofas. This month Johnson is having a big sale, so 3 delivery trucks will be coming to the store. How many sofas will they deliver?

   _____

2. There are 10 shelves of shoes in the back room of The Sports Center. Each shelf has the same number of shoes. There are 80 shoes on the 10 shelves. How many shoes are on one shelf?

   _____

3. Carmen is playing wheelchair basketball. You have to stay in the wheelchair the whole time you play the game. Carmen can roll her wheelchair down the court 12 feet in 2 seconds. How far can she go in 6 seconds?

   _____

4. The cost of gasoline is hitting record prices. It costs $4 for a gallon of gas during the summer when everyone wants to travel. How much will it cost to buy 15 gallons of gas?

   _____

5. Ramon's Music Store will buy used CDs from you at the price of 3 CDs for $10. You want to sell the store 12 CDs. What will they pay you?

   _____

Name _____ Date _____

Problem-Solving Activity
Finding the Measure of Two Angles

Write algebraic expressions to find the missing measures of the angles.

1. What is the measure of each angle? _____

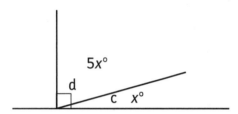

2. What is the measure of each angle? _____

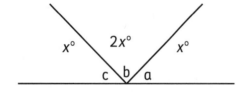

Name _____ Date _____

3. All of the angles measure $x°$. What is the measure of each angle?

    _____

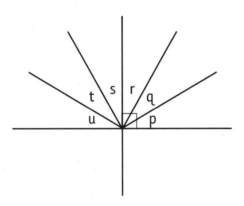

4. What is the measure of ∠j ? _____

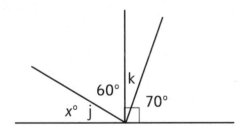

mBook Reinforce Understanding
Use the mBook *Study Guide* to review lesson concepts.

Unit 7 • Lesson 6 255

Unit 7

Name _____ Date _____

Skills Maintenance
Equations With Coefficients

Activity 1

Solve the problems with coefficients by using properties of equality and reciprocals.

1. $6a = 42$ _____

2. $7b = 49$ _____

3. $8c = 56$ _____

4. $9d = 81$ _____

Activity 2

Find the missing integers to complete the equations.

1. $-6 \cdot -9 =$ _____

2. $-27 = -3 \cdot$ _____

3. _____ $+ -12 = -13$

4. $17 -$ _____ $= 27$

5. $56 \div -8 =$ _____

6. $-100 +$ _____ $= -150$

Apply Skills

Equations With Negative Numbers

Name _____ **Date** _____

> **Activity 1**

Solve the equations involving negative variables and/or number terms.
Be sure to check your answers when you are finished using substitution.

1. $-5 - x + 5 + 5x = 12$ _____

Show your work here.

Check your answer here: _____

2. $x - 2 + -4 = -5$ _____

Show your work here.

Check your answer here: _____

3. $-10 + x - -5 = 10$ _____

Show your work here.

Check your answer here: _____

4. $3x - 4 - -4 + 2x = -15$ _____

Show your work here.

Check your answer here. _____

Name _____ Date _____

Problem-Solving Activity
Missing Angles in Triangles

Use what you know about the measures of common angles to solve the problems. Write algebraic equations to find each solution and be sure to show your work. Think about each problem before you try to solve it. Some problems require different strategies.

1. What are the measurements of ∠f, ∠g and ∠h?

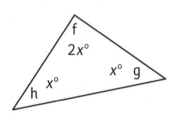

2. What are the measurements of ∠h, ∠j, and ∠k?

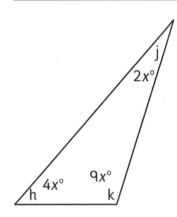

Name _____ Date _____

3. What are the measurements of ∠k, ∠l, and ∠m?

_____

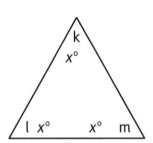

4. What are the measurements of ∠b, ∠m, and ∠x?

_____

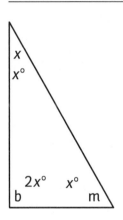

mBook **Reinforce Understanding**
Use the mBook *Study Guide* to review lesson concepts.

Name _____ Date _____

 Skills Maintenance
Solving Proportions

Activity 1

Use cross multiplication to solve the proportions.

Model	$\frac{4}{x} = \frac{2}{4}$ $2x = 16$ $x = \underline{\quad 8 \quad}$

1. $\frac{3}{4} = \frac{12}{w}$ $w =$ _____
   Show your work here.

2. $\frac{5}{x} = \frac{15}{18}$ $x =$ _____
   Show your work here.

3. $\frac{z}{8} = \frac{27}{72}$ $z =$ _____
   Show your work here.

Name _____ Date _____

 Apply Skills
Rate Problems and Algebra

Activity 1

Write a proportion to represent each of the rate problems. Use cross multiplication to solve the proportions. Be sure you are answering the question that the problem asks.

1. If it takes Jonah 15 minutes to run a mile, how long will it take him to run 3 miles at the same rate?

    Write the proportion. _____

    Solve the proportion. _____

    What is the answer to the problem?

    _____

2. If it takes Becca 10 minutes to read one page of her book, how long will it take her to read 5 pages at the same rate?

    Write the proportion. _____

    Solve the proportion. _____

    What is the answer to the problem?

    _____

3. If Eli can earn 100 points in 5 minutes on his video game, how many points can he earn in 20 minutes at the same rate?

    Write the proportion. _____

    Solve the proportion. _____

    What is the answer to the problem?

    _____

Unit 7

Name _____ Date _____

4. Marshall's Shipping Service moves goods up and down the East
    Coast. Their truck drivers work at night when there are fewer
    people on the freeway. Bill usually drives at 65 miles per hour, and
    he drives for 6 hours before he stops. How far does he drive before
    he stops?

    Write the proportion. _____

    Solve the proportion. _____

    What is the answer to the problem? _____

    _____

5. One night Juanita was driving from New York to Boston when she
    ran into bad weather. She averaged 50 miles per hour and she
    stopped for coffee and something to eat after 250 miles. How long
    did she drive?

    Write the proportion. _____

    Solve the proportion. _____

    What is the answer to the problem? _____

    _____

6. Marshall's also uses trains to ship goods long distances. Trains
    average a slower speed than trucks. They average 50 miles
    per hour, but trains don't stop as often as trucks. The train to
    Pittsburgh goes 12 hours before it stops. How many miles does
    it travel?

    Write the proportion. _____

    Solve the proportion. _____

    What is the answer to the problem? _____

    _____

7. When a train goes through the mountains, the speed drops even
    further. It can take 10 hours to go 300 miles. What is the rate of
    speed?

    Write the proportion. _____

    Solve the proportion. _____

    What is the answer to the problem? _____

    _____

Name _____ Date _____

✏️ Problem-Solving Activity
Triangles With Congruent Angles

Decide if the triangles have congruent sides or angles. Use algebraic expressions to find the measurements of all the angles.

1.

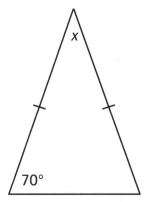

70°

Algebraic expression:

_____

2.

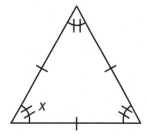

Algebraic expression:

_____

3.

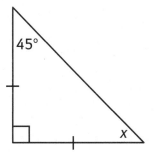

45°

Algebraic expression:

_____

4.

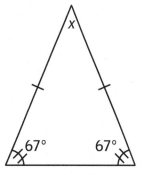

67°   67°

Algebraic expression:

_____

mBook **Reinforce Understanding**
Use the **mBook** *Study Guide* to review lesson concepts.

Name _____ Date _____

Skills Maintenance
Missing Angles

Activity 1

Use your knowledge of angles, properties, and algebraic expressions to find the missing angles.

1. What is the measure of angle *a*? _____

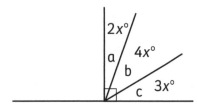

2. What is the measure of angle *m*? _____

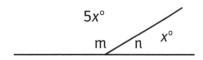

3. What is the measure of angle *h*? _____

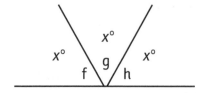

Name _____ Date _____

Apply Skills
Writing Equations From Words

Activity 1

Write algebraic expressions for each of the word statements. Use any of the four operations or inequality signs to write your expressions.

1. three times a number _____

2. three more than a number _____

3. a number less than 3 _____

4. the sum of 3 and a number times three _____

5. a number greater than 3 _____

Activity 2

Write algebraic equations for each of the word statements, then solve them.

1. Three times a number equals 180.

   Equation _____

   Solve _____

2. A number minus four equals twelve.

   Equation _____

   Solve _____

3. Two times a number equals negative ten.

   Equation _____

   Solve _____

4. A number minus negative three equals negative seven.

   Equation _____

   Solve _____

Name _____ Date _____

Problem-Solving Activity
Word Problems and Algebra

Translate each word problem into an algebraic expression and solve.

1. John makes three times as much as Allen per hour. Allen makes $7 per hour. How much does John make?

   _____

2. Randy's pet store carries two times less feed brands than Mandy's store. Randy has 14 kinds of feed. How many kinds does Mandy carry?

   _____

3. Rich can run three times as far as Mike in 4 hours. Rich can run 12 miles. How far can Mike run?

   _____

4. Lulu goes to the movie theater 17 times per month. Her friend Sarah goes to the movie theater 16 less time a month than Lulu. How many times does Sarah go to the movie theater per month?

   _____

5. Train trips that go from the East Coast to the middle of the country can take a long time because of delays. A recent trip averaged 45 miles per hour, and it traveled 900 miles. How long did this trip take?

   _____

6. Your friend and you are racing to see who can drive the 730 miles from Boston, Massachusetts to Raleigh, North Carolina first. It takes you 15 hours to get there. Your friend gets to Raleigh twice as fast. How long does it take your friend to get to Raleigh?

   _____

mBook Reinforce Understanding
Use the mBook *Study Guide* to review lesson concepts.

Name _____   Date _____

Skills Maintenance
Finding the Missing Angles

Activity 1

Find the missing angle measures.

1. What is the measurement of ∠a? _____

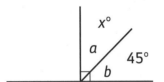

2. What is the measurement of ∠c? _____

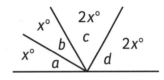

3. What are the measurements of ∠j and ∠k?

   j: _____   k: _____

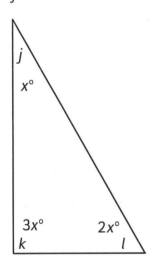

4. What are the measurements of ∠x and ∠y?

   x: _____   y: _____

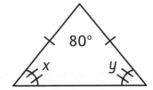

Name _____ Date _____

Unit Review
Introduction to Algebraic Expressions

Activity 1

Solve the problems by making sure each side of the equation is balanced. Be sure to show your work.

1. $x + 10 = 23 + 9$ _____   2. $3 + b - 8 = 15$ _____

3. $-4 + c + -6 = -20$ _____   4. $3 \cdot 5 + s = 4 \cdot 2 + 16$ _____

5. $4d = 60$ _____   6. $-3f = 15$ _____

7. $-5x = -20$ _____   8. $4v = 28 - 4 + 8$ _____

Activity 2

Solve the word problems using algebra. Be sure to show all of your work.

1. A recipe for cake calls for 2 cups of flour and 4 eggs. You want to make a cake that uses 12 eggs. How much flour should you use?

   _____

2. Your teacher is passing out tests and pencils for an exam. She wants there to be 3 pencils for every 1 exam. If she passes out 98 tests, how many pencils does she need?

   _____

3. Katie and Ali and running to see who can get to their car first. Katie runs the 500 meters in 20 seconds. If Ali gets there twice as fast, how many seconds will it take her?

   _____

Name _____ Date _____

Unit Review
Geometric Construction and Angle Measurement

Activity 1

Use a compass and a ruler to construct a perpendicular line, then bisect the angle.

1. Use line segment FG to create a perpendicular line segment.

F   G

2. Bisect this angle.

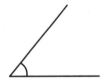

Name _____ Date _____

Activity 2

Use this information and your knowledge of angle properties to find the missing angle in each problem. Answer the problem using an algebraic equation. Show all of your work.

1. What is the measure of ∠v? _____

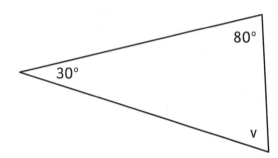

Show your work here:

2. What is the measure of ∠g? _____

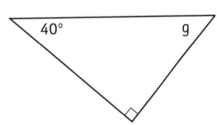

Show your work here:

3. What is the measure of ∠m? _____

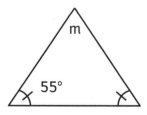

Show your work here:

Name _____ Date _____

4. What is the measure of ∠t? _____

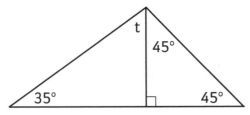

5. What is the measure of ∠z? _____

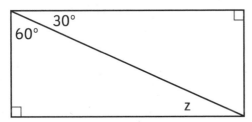

6. What is the measure of ∠f? What is the measure of ∠g?

f _____ g _____

Name _____ Date _____

Skills Maintenance
Solving Equations

Activity 1

Solve the equations using the properties and rules you know. Check the answer when you are done by substituting the value for the variable in the original equation.

Model	$x - 9 = 15$ Solve: $\quad x + -9 = 15$ $\quad\quad x + -9 + 9 = 15 + 9$ $\quad\quad\quad x + 0 = 24$ $\quad\quad\quad\quad x = \underline{24}$ Check: $\quad 24 - 9 = 15$ $\quad\quad\quad 15 = 15$ TRUE

1. $x + 7 = 24$

Solve:

$x =$ _____

Check:

2. $w - 3 = -2$

Solve:

$w =$ _____

Check:

3. $-3z = 24$

Solve:

$z =$ _____

Check:

4. $4y = 36$

Solve:

$y =$ _____

Check:

Name _____ Date _____

%÷ Apply Skills
Thinking About Algebraic Equations

Activity 1

Look at the pairs of equations. There is a slight difference in each of them. Circle the part that is different.

Model	$3x + 2 - 3 \boxed{(+\ 5)} = 10$
	$3x + 2 - 3 \boxed{(-\ 5)} = 10$

1. $x + 2 + -3 + 5 = 20$

   $x + 2 + 3 + 5 = 20$

2. $24 = 3x + 5 - -3 - x$

   $24 = 3x + 5 - -3 + x$

3. $3x - 9 + 2 = 35$

   $-3x - 9 + 2 = 35$

4. $-17 = -x - 3 - 5 - -2$

   $-17 = -x - 3 + 5 - -2$

Activity 2

There is a slight difference between the two equations in each pair. Solve each equation and be ready to compare and discuss the answers. Show your work.

1. $3x - x + 2x = 8$ and $-3x - x + 2x = 8$

2. $-5 + x - 7 = 24$ and $5 + x - 7 = 24$

3. $-17 + x + 17 + -1 = 2$ and $-17 + x + 17 + 1 = 2$

Unit 8

Name _____ Date _____

Problem-Solving Activity
Interior Angle Measurement of Regular Polygons

Use the pattern in the *Table of Measures for Regular Polygons* in the *Student Text* to solve the problems. In some cases, you will have to draw triangles in the shape in order to find out how many there are. Then write three equations for each shape.

1. Hexagon

Three algebraic equations for a hexagon

_____

_____

_____

2. Octagon

Three algebraic equations for an octagon

_____

_____

_____

Name _____ Date _____

3. Pentagon

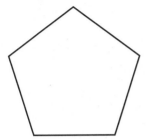

Three algebraic equations for a pentagon

_____

_____

_____

4. Nonagon

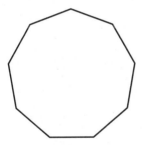

Three algebraic equations for a nonagon

_____

_____

_____

mBook **Reinforce Understanding**
Use the mBook *Study Guide* to review lesson concepts.

Unit 8 • Lesson 1   **275**

Name _____ Date _____

 Skills Maintenance
Multiplying Integers

Activity 1

Complete the equations. Remember the PASS rules.

1. $-1 \cdot 3 =$ _____

2. $4 \cdot$ _____ $= -4$

3. $-7 =$ _____ $\cdot -1$

4. $-2 \cdot -1 =$ _____

5. $-1 \cdot$ _____ $= -8$

6. $-12 =$ _____ $\cdot 12$

Name _____ Date _____

 Apply Skills
Invisible Coefficients

Activity 1

Solve the equations involving invisible coefficients. Show all of your work so you can analyze the steps later if you make a mistake.

1. $-a = -25$

    Show your work here:

2. $b - 2b = 12$

    Show your work here:

3. $-27 = -3c + -6c$

    Show your work here:

4. $-d = 5 + -5$

    Show your work here:

5. $e + 2e + -4e = -5$

    Show your work here:

Unit 8

Name _____ Date _____

Problem-Solving Activity
Exterior Angle Measurement of Regular Polygons

In the *Table of Measures for Regular Polygons* you will find the measure of interior angles for different regular polygons. Use this information to solve the problems. Find the sum of the measure of exterior angles for different polygons. You will also write two equations:

1. An equation for the exterior angle.

2. An equation for the sum of the exterior angles.

Table of Measures for Regular Polygons			
Shape	Number of Sides	Total Measure of the Interior Angles	Measure of Each Angle
triangle	3	180°	60°
square	4	360°	90°
pentagon	5	540°	108°
hexagon	6	720°	120°
octagon	8	1,080°	135°

1. Hexagon

2. Octagon

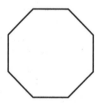

Write an equation for the exterior angle of a hexagon.

_____

$n =$ _____

Write an equation for the sum of the exterior angles of a hexagon.

_____

$n =$ _____

Write an equation for the exterior angle of an octagon.

_____

$n =$ _____

Write an equation for the sum of the exterior angles of an octagon.

_____

$c =$ _____

Name _____ Date _____

3. Pentagon

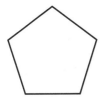

Write an equation for the exterior angle of a pentagon.

_____

$n =$ _____

Write an equation for the sum of the exterior angles of a pentagon.

_____

$j =$ _____

4. Square

Write an equation for the exterior angle of a square.

_____

$n =$ _____

Write an equation for the sum of the exterior angles of a square.

_____

$s =$ _____

Name _____ Date _____

 Skills Maintenance
Evaluating Expressions

Activity 1

Evaluate the expressions. Select the correct answer.

1. $3 + {-2} \cdot 5$

    (a) -7

    (b) 7

    (c) 6

2. $-1 \cdot 4 + 7$

    (a) -11

    (b) 3

    (c) 11

3. $-7 - 42 \div 7$

    (a) 7

    (b) -13

    (c) -7

4. $4 - 8 + 4$

    (a) -8

    (b) 16

    (c) 0

Name _____ Date _____

%÷ **Apply Skills**
Multistep Equations

Activity 1

Solve the equations. Show all of the steps involved. Check your work by substituting the value for the variable back into the original equation.

1. $3x + 9 = 27$

    Show your work here:

    $x =$ _____

    Check your work here:

2. $4x - 12 = 24$

    Show your work here:

    $x =$ _____

    Check your work here:

3. $-3 + -4 + 6x = 35$

    Show your work here:

    $x =$ _____

    Check your work here:

4. $-2x - 3 + 5 = -10$

    $x =$ _____

    Check your work here:

Unit 8

Name _____ Date _____

Problem-Solving Activity
Angle Measurement of Irregular Polygons

Use the table *Polygons and the Sums of the Measures of Interior and Exterior Angles* from the *Student Text* to solve the problems. Make sure you write an algebraic equation to solve each problem.

1.

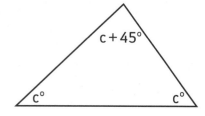

_____

2.

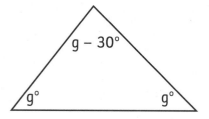

_____

3.

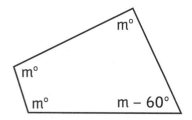

_____

 Reinforce Understanding
Use the mBook *Study Guide* to review lesson concepts.

Name _____ Date _____

Skills Maintenance
Multistep Equations

Activity 1

Solve the multistep equations. Show your work. Use subtraction to check your answers.

1. $3x + 5 = 20$

    Show your work here:

    $x =$ _____

    Check your work here:

2. $45 - 5 = -8x$

    Show your work here:

    $x =$ _____

    Check your work here:

Name _____ Date _____

%÷ Apply Skills
Translating Numbers into Equations

Write the number patterns using algebraic equations. You may need two variables.

Model	The numeric pattern is: $3 + -3 = 0 \quad 4 + -4 = 0 \quad 5 + -5 = 0$ Write the equation. $\underline{x + -x = 0}$

1. The numeric pattern is:

    $5 \cdot -1 = -5$

    $6 \cdot -1 = -6$

    $7 \cdot -1 = -7$

    Write the equation.

    _____

2. The numeric pattern is:

    $0 = -5 \cdot 0$

    $0 = 27 \cdot 0$

    $0 = 1{,}437.5 \cdot 0$

    Write the equation.

    _____

3. The numeric pattern is:

    $3 \cdot 4 = 4 \cdot 3$

    $100 \cdot 10 = 10 \cdot 100$

    $-5 \cdot -4 = -4 \cdot -5$

    Write the equation.

    _____

4. The numeric pattern is:

    $5 (3 + 2) = 5 \cdot 3 + 5 \cdot 2$

    $-2 (7 + 1) = -2 \cdot 7 + -2 \cdot 1$

    $18 (1 + 2) = 18 \cdot 1 + 18 \cdot 2$

    Write the equation.

    _____

5. The numeric pattern is:

    $3 + 5 + -5 = 3 + 0$

    $4 + 6 + -6 = 4 + 0$

    $17 + 22 + -22 = 17 + 0$

    Write the equation.

    _____

6. The numeric pattern is:

    $-3 \cdot -1 = 3$

    $-100 \cdot -1 = 100$

    $-4.5 \cdot -1 = 4.5$

    Write the equation.

    _____

Name _____ Date _____

Activity 2

Think about the relationship between numbers as you answer the problems. Make sure to check your answer by substituting the values into the original equation.

1. Two numbers add up to 100. The larger number is three times greater than the smaller number. What are the two numbers? _____

2. Two numbers add up to 56. The larger number is 10 greater than the smaller number. What are the two numbers? _____

3. Two numbers add up to 30. One number is 4 less than the other number. What are the two numbers? _____

4. Two numbers add up to 90. One number is 5 times greater than the other number. What are the two numbers? _____

5. Three numbers add up to 70. The first number is 10 more than the second number. The second number is the same as the third number. What are the three numbers? _____

mBook Reinforce Understanding
Use the mBook *Study Guide* to review lesson concepts.

Unit 8

Name _____ Date _____

 ## Skills Maintenance
Writing Equations to Solve Word Problems

Activity 1

Write the equation that you would use to solve each of the word problems. You do not need to solve the problem.

Model	If the difference between two numbers is 60 and one number is 4 times bigger than the other number, what are the two numbers? Write the equation. $4x - x = 60$

1. If the sum of two numbers is 150 and one number is 20 more than the other number, what are the two numbers?

    Write the equation. _____

2. If the sum of four numbers is 100 and each of the numbers is the same, what are the four numbers?

    Write the equation. _____

3. If the difference of two numbers is 500 and one number is three times greater than the other number, what are the two numbers?

    Write the equation. _____

Name _____ Date _____

Problem-Solving Activity
Angles of Quadrilaterals

Tell if there is enough information to find the missing angle measures. If there is enough information, use algebra to find the missing angle measures.

1.

Is there enough information to find the measure of x?

(circle)   YES   or   NO

If there is enough information, write the equation.

_____

Solve the equation.

What is the measure of angle x? _____

2.

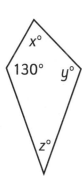

Is there enough information to find the measure of angle z?

(circle)   YES   or   NO

If there is enough information, write the equation.

_____

Solve the equation.

What is the measure of angle z? _____

3.

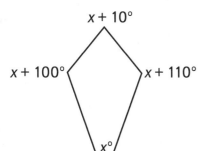

Is there enough information to find the measure of angle x?

(circle)   YES   or   NO

If there is enough information, write the equation.

_____

Solve the equation.

What is the measure of angle x?

Name _____ Date _____

Skills Maintenance
Angles of Quadrilaterals

Activity 1

Find the missing angle.

1.

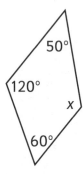

What is the measure of angle *x*? _____

2.

What is the measure of angle *a*? _____

3.

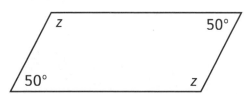

What is the measure of the angles labeled angle *z*? _____

Integer Multiplication

Activity 2

Solve the problems involving multiplication of integers.

1. $-1 \cdot -3 =$ _____

2. $-5 \cdot$ _____ $= -45$

3. _____ $= -7 \cdot 3$

4. $-3 \cdot -5 =$ _____

Name _____ Date _____

Apply Skills
Negative Coefficients

Activity 1

Solve each pair of equations. Pay close attention to the negative signs. Compare the answers. Write about the different steps that you used because of the negative sign. Write about the difference in the answers.

1. Solve the two equations: $2x = 6$ $-2x = 6$

    Show your work here:

    Compare the steps you used to solve each. How are they alike and how are they different?

    _____

    _____

    _____

    Compare answers. What is the difference in the answer?

    _____

    _____

    _____

Unit 8

Name _____ Date _____

2. Solve the two equations: $x + 5 = 14$ $-x + 5 = 14$

Show your work here:

Compare the steps you used to solve each. How are they alike and how are they different?

_____

_____

_____

Compare answers. What is the difference in your answer?

_____

_____

_____

3. Solve the two equations: $2x + 4 = 20$ $-2x - 4 = 20$

Show your work here:

Compare the steps you used to solve each. How are they alike and how are they different?

_____

_____

_____

Compare answers. What is the difference in the answer?

_____

_____

_____

Name _____ Date _____

Problem-Solving Activity
Using Drawings to Solve Problems

Use drawings to set up the problems. Then follow the steps to solve each problem. Make sure that you answer what the problem is asking for.

1. There are three stacks of dollar bills on the counter. The second stack has 5 times the number of bills as the first stack. The third stack has 2 times the number of bills as the first stack. When you count all of the money, the total amount is $160. How much money is in each stack?

    _____

2. It is time to pay bills. Carmen writes three checks. The second check is 4 times the amount of the first check. The third check is 3 times the amount of the first check. The total amount for all three checks is $200. How much is written on each check?

    _____

3. Hector's younger sister saves pennies in jars. She has two jars with pennies. The first jar has 10 times more pennies than the second jar. Combined, she has 55 pennies. How many pennies are in each jar?

    _____

Name _____ Date _____

4. Laura and Dana are both working as servers in a restaurant. At the end of the shift, they count their tips. Laura has 2 times minus $5 as much money in tips than Dana. Combined they have $40. How much money does each one have in tips?

_____

5. There are two cash registers in the store. The second cash register has 3 times the amount of money as the first cash register plus $10. The total amount of money in the two cash registers is $90. How much money is in each cash register?

_____

mBook Reinforce Understanding
Use the mBook *Study Guide* to review lesson concepts.

Name _____ Date _____

Skills Maintenance
Equations With Integers

Activity 1

Solve the problems.

1. $-2x = -16$

    Show your work here:

    $x = $ _____

    Check your work here:

2. $-3x - -4 = -8$

    Show your work here:

    $x = $ _____

    Check your work here:

Angles of Quadrilaterals

Activity 2

Tell the measure of the missing angle in the quadrilaterals. Remember, the sum of the interior angles for parallelograms is always 360 degrees.

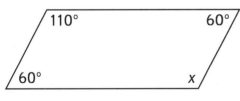

1. 110°   60°
    60°   x

    Angle $x = $ _____

2. y

    Angle $y = $ _____

Unit 8

Name _____ Date _____

 Apply Skills
Variables on Both Sides of the Equal Sign

Activity 1

Solve the equations that have variables on both sides of the equal sign. Show all of your work. Check your answer by substituting the value back into the original equation.

Model	
	$3x - 6 = x + 8$
	$-x + 3x - 6 = -x + x + 8$
	$2x - 6 = 8$
	$2x - 6 + 6 = 8 + 6$
	$2x = 14$
	$x = 7$

1. $4x + -2 = -2x + 4$

    Show your work here:

    $x = $ _____

    Check your work here:

2. $3 + x = -2 + x + x$

    Show your work here:

    $x = $ _____

    Check your work here:

Name _____ Date _____

3. $6x - 4 = -4x + 36$

Show your work here:

$x =$ _____

Check your work here:

4. $-2 - 6 - x = -2x - 6$

Show your work here:

$x =$ _____

Check your work here:

Name _____ Date _____

Problem-Solving Activity
Using Drawings to Solve Rate Problems

Draw pictures to help you set up the problems. Then follow the steps you learned in this lesson to solve each problem. Remember that these problems are based on the formula $r \cdot t = d$. Make sure that you answer what the problem is asking.

1. Two cars start out in two different cities. The cities are 270 miles apart. The cars are driving toward each other on the same road. The first car's speed is 50 miles per hour. The second car's speed is 40 miles per hour. How long before they meet? _____

2. Jing and Maya are riding their bikes. They start at Jing's house, but they go opposite directions. Both are going the same speed and they ride for 2 hours. At the end of that time, they are 40 miles apart. How fast are they riding (in miles per hour)?

   _____

Name _____ Date _____

3. Bill and Carl are running a race for cancer. Each person gets $3 for every mile he runs. Bill is running 8 miles per hour and Carl is running 12 miles per hour. How long will they have to run before they run a total of 60 miles between the two of them? _____

4. Two space satellites are going to crash into each other in their next orbit around Earth. They are now 5,000 miles apart. The first satellite is traveling 200 miles per minute and the second satellite is traveling 300 miles per minute. How many minutes until they crash? _____

5. Howard's water pipes froze under his house during the winter. When it warmed up, he had two big leaks. One leaked at a rate of 3 gallons per hour and the second at a rate of 1 gallon per hour. How long did it take before 20 gallons of water leaked from his pipes? _____

mBook Reinforce Understanding
Use the mBook *Study Guide* to review lesson concepts.

Name _____ Date _____

 Skills Maintenance
Equations With Variables on Both Sides

Activity 1

Solve each equation.

1. $2x + 5 = 3x + 5$

   Show your work here:

   $x =$ _____

   Check your work here:

2. $-6 + x = 2x - 5$

   Show your work here:

   $x =$ _____

   Check your work here:

Activity 2

Rewrite each pattern using an equation with variables that represent the pattern.

Model	$6 + 2 = 2 + 6$ $8 + 5 = 5 + 8$ $-1 + -2 = -2 + -1$ Write the equation. $\underline{x + y = y + x}$

1. $3(4 + 2) = 3 \cdot 4 + 3 \cdot 2$

   $2(5 + 1) = 2 \cdot 5 + 2 \cdot 1$

   $6(8 + 2) = 6 \cdot 8 + 6 \cdot 2$

   Write the equation. _____

2. $4 \cdot 1 + 4 \cdot 9 = 4(1 + 9)$

   $2 \cdot 3 + 2 \cdot 8 = 2(3 + 8)$

   $6 \cdot 5 + 6 \cdot 6 = 6(5 + 6)$

   Write the equation. _____

Name _____ Date _____

Apply Skills
The Distributive Property in Equations

Activity 1

Solve the equations using the distributive property. Be sure to show your work and check your answers.

1. $3(x + 5) = 30$

    Show your work here:

    $x =$ _____

    Check your work here:

2. $2(x + 10) = 40$

    Show your work here:

    $x =$ _____

    Check your work here:

3. $-2(-x + -1) = -12$

    Show your work here:

    $x =$ _____

    Check your work here:

Unit 8

Name _____ Date _____

Problem-Solving Activity
Angles and Intersecting Lines

Use algebra to find the total measurement of the exterior angles for each figure. Look for a pattern in the measures of these angles. Can you make a general statement about the measure of angles in straight lines that intersect?

1. What are the measures of ∠2, ∠3, and ∠4?

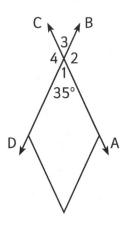

_____

2. What are the measures of ∠1, ∠2, and ∠3?

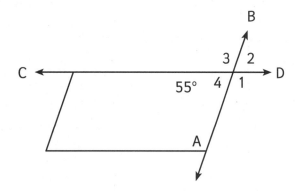

_____

Name _____ Date _____

3. What are the measures of ∠2, ∠3, and ∠4?

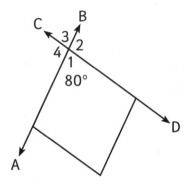

_____

4. What are the measures of ∠1, ∠2, and ∠3?

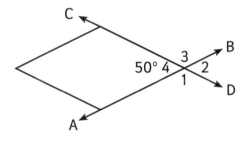

_____

mBook **Reinforce Understanding**
Use the **mBook** *Study Guide* to review lesson concepts.

Unit 8

Unit 8 • Lesson 8   **301**

Name _____ Date _____

Skills Maintenance
Distributive Property

Activity 1

Solve the equations using the distributive property. Be sure to show your work and check your answers.

1. $2(-x - 4) = 16$

Show your work here:

$x =$ _____

Check your work here:

2. $-x(3 + 4) = 14$

Show your work here:

$x =$ _____

Check your work here:

Activity 2

Solve the multiplication problems with fractions.

1. $\frac{1}{3} \cdot 3 =$ _____

2. $\frac{3}{5} \cdot$ _____ $= 1$

3. $\frac{4}{5} \cdot \frac{5}{4} =$ _____

4. $1 = \frac{2}{3} \cdot$ _____

5. _____ $\cdot \frac{1}{3} = 1$

6. $\frac{1}{2} \cdot$ _____ $= 1$

7. $8 \cdot$ _____ $= 1$

8. $\frac{11}{12} \cdot \frac{12}{11} =$ _____

Name _____ Date _____

 Apply Skills

Flexibility and the Distributive Property

Activity 1

Solve the equations. Show your work and check your answers.

1. $-2(3 + x) = 12$

    Show your work here:

    $x =$ _____

    Check your work here:

2. $3(-z - 1) = -12$

    Show your work here:

    $z =$ _____

    Check your work here:

3. $4(y - 1) = 16$

    Show your work here:

    $y =$ _____

    Check your work here:

Name _____ Date _____

Activity 2

For each of the problems on the previous page, select a different strategy to solve the equations again. Explain how the steps are different.

1. Solve $-2(3 + x) = 12$ in a different way than you solved it in Activity 1.

   Show your work here:

   $x =$ _____

   Check your work here:

   Tell how the steps are different:

   _____

   _____

   _____

2. Solve $3(-z - 1) = -12$ in a different way than you solved it in Activity 1.

   Show your work here:

   $z =$ _____

   Check your work here:

   Tell how the steps are different:

   _____

   _____

   _____

3. Solve $4(y - 1) = 16$ using a different method.

   Show your work here:

   $y =$ _____

   Check your work here:

   Tell how the steps are different:

   _____

   _____

   _____

Name _____ Date _____

Problem-Solving Activity
Angles and Parallel Lines

Use what you have learned about vertical angles and corresponding angles to solve the problems. All lines in the problems are parallel.

1. What is the measure of ∠6? _____

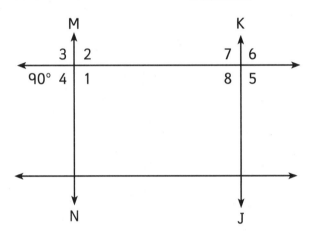

2. What is the measure of ∠8? _____

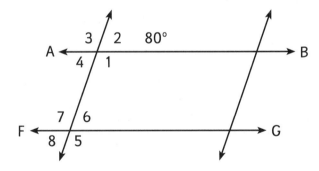

Name _____ Date _____

3. What is the measure of ∠2? _____

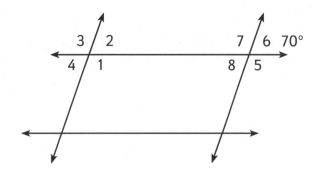

4. What is the measure of ∠3? _____

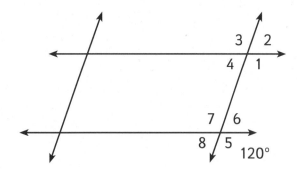

mBook **Reinforce Understanding**
Use the **mBook** *Study Guide* to review lesson concepts.

306 Unit 8 • Lesson 9

Name _____ Date _____

Skills Maintenance
Vertical and Corresponding Angles

Activity 1

Use the diagram to answer the questions about angles.

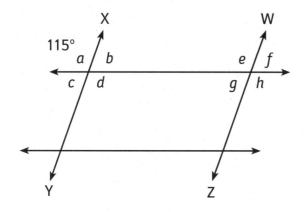

1. ∠a and ∠b are _____ angles.

2. If you know that the measure of ∠a is 115°, what is the measure of ∠d? _____

3. What kinds of angles are ∠a and ∠d? _____

4. Explain why the measures of ∠b and ∠f are the same.

   _____

5. What is the measure of ∠c? _____

6. What is the measure of ∠g? _____

Unit 8

Name _____ Date _____

%÷ Apply Skills
Area Formulas and Algebra Equations

Find the missing measure in each shape using area formulas and the distributive property.

1. If the area of this shape is 32 square units, what is the measure of its base? _____

   Show your work here:

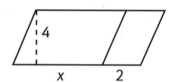

   If the base is represented with the expression $x + 2$, what is the measure of x? _____

2. If the area of this shape is 24 square units, what is the measure of its base? _____

   Show your work here:

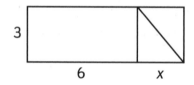

   If the base is represented with the expression $6 + x$, what is the measure of x? _____

3. If the area of this shape is 48 square units, what is the measure of the height? _____

   Show your work here:

   If the height is represented with the expression $8 + x$, what is the measure of x? _____

Name _____ Date _____

 Skills Maintenance
Area Formulas and Algebra

Activity 1

Use algebra and common area formulas to solve the problems.

1. What is the area of this triangle? The formula is
   $A = \frac{1}{2} \cdot b \cdot h$ _____

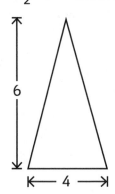

2. What is the measure of the base of this rectangle if its area is
   20 square units? The formula is $A = b \cdot h$ _____

3. What is the measure of the height of this rectangle if the area is
   27 square units? _____

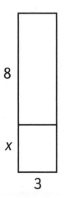

Unit 8

Name _____ Date _____

%÷/=/<x **Apply Skills**
Commutative and Associative Properties

Activity 1

Solve the problems using the properties you learned to simplify your work.

1. $2x - 4 + 7 - 8 + x + 3x + 4 = -7$

   Simplify the equation here:

   Solve the simplified equation here:

   $x =$ _____

   Check your work here:

2. $-2 = 3 + x + 4 + -x + x - 4$

   Simplify the equation here:

   Solve the simplified equation here:

   $x =$ _____

   Check your work here:

3. $2x + 4 = -5 + x + 7 + 2x + -2 - 1$

   Simplify the equation here:

   Solve the simplified equation here:

   $x =$ _____

   Check your work here:

4. $4 + 5 - 3 - 1 + 2x - 4 = x + 1$

   Simplify the equation here:

   Solve the simplified equation here:

   $x =$ _____

   Check your work here:

Name _____ Date _____

Problem-Solving Activity
Proving Angles Are Equal

Use the vertical and corresponding angles rules, as well as the transitive property, to solve the problems. Be sure to write the reasons for each step in your proof.

1. Lines PQ and XY are parallel. Prove that $\angle 3$ and $\angle 5$ are equal.

    _____

    _____

    _____

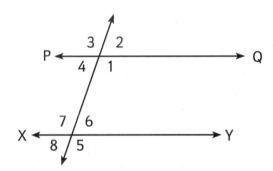

2. Lines RS and TU are parallel. Prove that $\angle 4$ and $\angle 6$ are equal.

    _____

    _____

    _____

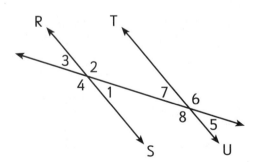

Name _____ Date _____

3. Lines RS and TU are parallel. Lines WX and YZ are parallel. Prove that ∠1 and ∠7 are equal.

    _____

    _____

    _____

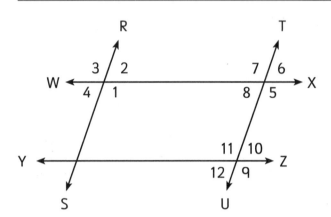

4. Lines EF and KM are parallel. Lines WX and YZ are parallel. Prove that ∠4 and ∠10 are equal.

    _____

    _____

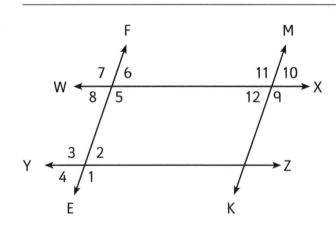

mBook **Reinforce Understanding**
Use the **mBook** *Study Guide* to review lesson concepts.

Name _____ Date _____

Skills Maintenance
Solving Complex Equations

Activity 1

Solve the equations. Be sure to simplify first. Check your answers when you are done.

1. $-5x + 7 + -4x + 2 = 18$

    Show your work here:

    $x =$ _____

    Check your work here:

2. $-35 = 3x + -x - 65 - 5 + 5x$

    Show your work here:

    $x =$ _____

    Check your work here:

Name _____ Date _____

%÷ Apply Skills
≡=x
<x Fractions as Coefficients

> **Activity 1**

Solve the equations that have fractions as coefficients.

1. $\frac{1}{2}x + 34 = 48$

   Show your work here:

   $x =$ _____

   Check your work here:

2. $\frac{1}{3}(x + 3) = 9$

   Show your work here:

   $x =$ _____

   Check your work here:

3. $40 = \frac{2}{3}x + -34$

   Show your work here:

   $x =$ _____

   Check your work here:

Name _____ Date _____

Problem-Solving Activity
Making Inferences in Geometry

Use what you know about the measure of angles, shapes, and the rules and properties described below to solve the problems.

> **Right angles**— ⌐ this symbols shows that an angle is always a right angle. The measure of a right angle is 90°.
>
> **Supplementary angles**—When you combine two angles to form a straight line, you have supplementary angles. A straight line measures 180°.
>
> **Vertical angles rule**—These are two angles whose sides are opposite rays. Vertical angles have equal measurement.
>
> **Corresponding angle rule**—When parallel lines are crossed by a transversal, corresponding angles have equal measurement.
>
> **Transitive property**—This is a property that shows relationships between quantities. If A = B and B = C, then A = C.

1. Find the measure of ∠15. _____

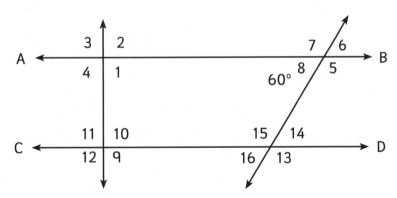

2. Find the measure of ∠2. _____

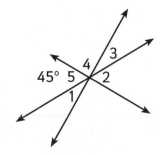

Name _____ Date _____

3. Find the measure of ∠16. _____

Lines AB and CD are parallel

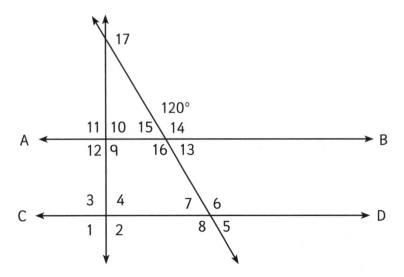

4. Find the measure of ∠14. _____

Lines JK and LM are parallel

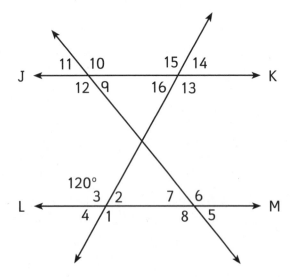

mBook **Reinforce Understanding**
Use the mBook *Study Guide* to review lesson concepts.

Name _____ Date _____

Skills Maintenance
Reciprocals

Activity 1

Tell the reciprocal for each number.

Model	What is the reciprocal of 3?
	Remember that 3 may be written as $\frac{3}{1}$.
	The reciprocal of 3 is ___$\frac{1}{3}$___ .

1. What is the reciprocal of 4? _____

2. What is the reciprocal of $\frac{1}{4}$? _____

3. What is the reciprocal of $\frac{2}{3}$? _____

4. What is the reciprocal of 10? _____

Inferences About Angles

Activity 2

Lines XY and WZ are parallel. Find the missing angle measures.

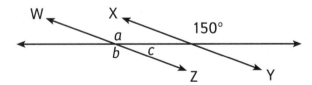

1. What is the measure of $\angle a$? _____

2. What is the measure of $\angle b$? _____

3. What is the measure of $\angle c$? _____

Unit 8

Name _____ Date _____

 Apply Skills
More on Fractions as Coefficients

> **Activity 1**

Convert each of the fractions by writing them as a product of 1 over the denominator and the numerator over 1.

Model	$\frac{3}{2} = \frac{1}{2} \cdot \frac{3}{1}$

1. $\frac{4}{5}$ = _____ • _____

2. $\frac{2}{3}$ = _____ • _____

3. $\frac{8}{9}$ = _____ • _____

4. $\frac{3}{4}$ = _____ • _____

Name _____ Date _____

Activity 2

Solve the equations. Rewrite the fraction as the product of 1 over the denominator and the numerator over 1.

Model

$$\frac{x+1}{2} = 12$$

Answer $\quad \frac{1}{2}(x+1) = 12$

$$2 \cdot \frac{1}{2}(x+1) = 12 \cdot 2$$

$$x + 1 = 24$$

$$x + 1 - 1 = 24 - 1$$

$$x + 0 = 23$$

$$x = 23$$

Check $\quad \frac{23+1}{2} = 12 \rightarrow \frac{24}{2} = 12 \rightarrow 12 = 12$ TRUE

---

1. $\frac{x}{5} = 5$

Rewrite the problem as 1 over the denominator and the numerator over 1:

_____

Solve the equation. Show your work here:

$x =$ _____

Check your work here:

2. $\frac{x+1}{2} = 2$

Rewrite the problem as 1 over the denominator and the numerator over 1:

_____

Solve the equation. Show your work here:

$x =$ _____

Check your work here:

Name _____ Date _____

3. $\dfrac{y+6}{6} = 3$

Rewrite the problem as 1 over the denominator and the numerator over 1:

_____

Solve the equation. Show your work here:

$y = $ _____

Check your work here:

4. $\dfrac{z+3}{4} = 10$

Rewrite the problem as 1 over the denominator and the numerator over 1:

_____

Solve the equation. Show your work here:

$z = $ _____

Check your work here:

Name _____ Date _____

 ## Problem-Solving Activity
Word Problems

Solve the age problems. Use these four steps to help you solve
each problem:

1. **Begin with a drawing.**
2. **Figure out how to use a variable.**
3. **Solve the equation.**
4. **Make sure the answer is what the question is asking for.**

1. Niki is 2 years younger than her brother Michael. When you
    combine their ages, it totals 38. How old are Niki and Michael?

    _____

2. Jordan is Randall's father. Jordan is 4 times older than Randall.
    When you add their ages together, it is 50. How old are Jordan and
    Randall?

    _____

3. Sherilyn has a much older cousin, Alisa, who lives in another city.
    Alisa is twice as old as Sherilyn. When you combine their ages it
    totals 24. How old are Sherilyn and Alisa?

    _____

Name _____ Date _____

4. Kara is 8 years older than Leah. In 10 more years, the total of their ages will be 28. How old are Kara and Leah?

_____

5. Robert is 5 years older than Josh. Danny is 8 years older than Josh. Their total age is 43. How old are Robert, Josh, and Danny?

_____

mBook **Reinforce Understanding**
Use the mBook *Study Guide* to review lesson concepts.

Name _____ Date _____

Skills Maintenance
Values of Coins as Equations

Activity 1

Add coins and tell the amount of money you have.

1. How much money is this?

_____

2. How much money is this?

_____

Missing Angle Measures

Activity 2

Find the missing angle measurements. Use the given information, rules, properties, and inferences.

1. What is the value of ∠a? _____

2. What is the value of ∠d? _____

3. What is the value of ∠f? _____

4. What is the value of ∠p? _____

Unit 8

Name _____ Date _____

Apply Skills
Negative Numbers

Activity 1

Solve the equations. Pay close attention to the negative numbers.

1. $-3 + -x = -12$

   Show your work here:

   $x =$ _____

   Check your answer here:

2. $-x - -5 = -7$

   Show your work here:

   $x =$ _____

   Check your answer here:

3. $-2x - 4 + 8 = 12$

   Show your work here:

   $x =$ _____

   Check your answer here:

4. $-4 - 7x = -32$

   Show your work here:

   $x =$ _____

   Check your answer here:

Name _____ Date _____

 Problem-Solving Activity
Coin Problems

Solve the coin problems using the four steps. Remember that you need to use the value of each coin when you make an equation. This is what makes coin problems a little different from other kinds of algebraic word problems.

1. **Begin with a drawing.**
2. **Figure out how to use a variable.**
3. **Solve the equation.**
4. **Make sure the answer is what the question is asking for.**

1.   I have 3 nickels and some dimes in the pants that I left on the floor of my bedroom. I remember that I had 85 cents in the pocket of those pants. How many dimes did I have? _____

2.   I thought that I took all of the money out of my desk drawer but I found 28 cents in it yesterday. I had 3 pennies and some nickels. How many nickels did I have? _____

3.   It turns out that I counted wrong when I looked in my desk drawer. I only had 22 cents. I had twice as many nickels as I had pennies. How many nickels and pennies did I have?

_____

Name _____ Date _____

4. I needed to borrow some money for lunch from a friend at school. He gave me all of the change in his pocket. When I counted it, the total was 53 cents. There was one quarter, one dime, one nickel, and a bunch of pennies. How many pennies were there? _____

5. Your turn. Make your own word problem using coins. Write the equation that goes along with the problem.

_____

_____

_____

_____

_____

_____

_____

mBook **Reinforce Understanding**
Use the mBook *Study Guide* to review lesson concepts.

Name _____ Date _____

 ### Skills Maintenance
Solving Complex Equations

Activity 1

Solve the equations. Be sure to simplify first, and then solve the simplified equation. Check your answers when you are done.

1. $4x - 2 + 6 - 5x = 10 + -3 + 2x$ $x =$ _____

    Show your work here:

    Check your work here:

2. $5 + -6 - 3x = 10x + 15 + 3x$ $x =$ _____

    Show your work here:

    Check your work here:

Unit 8

Name _____ Date _____

Unit Review
Solving Different Kinds of Algebraic Expressions

Activity 1

Solve the algebraic expressions. Some problems involve fractions with variables. Show all of your work.

1. $4x + 5 = 65$ $x =$ _____

   Show your work here:

   Check your answer here:

2. $-3x - 7 = 20$ $x =$ _____

   Show your work here:

   Check your work here:

3. $2x - 3 = x + 7$ $x =$ _____

   Show your work here:

   Check your work here:

4. $\frac{1}{3}x = 10$ $x =$ _____

   Check your work here:

Name _____ Date _____

5. $\frac{x}{2} + 1 = 9$ $x =$ _____

Show your work here:

Check your work here:

6. $-\frac{x}{2} + 1 = 9$ $x =$ _____

Show your work here:

Check your work here:

7. $9x - 3 = 15$ $x =$ _____

Show your work here:

Check your work here:

8. $3x - 5 = -23$ $x =$ _____

Show your work here:

Check your work here:

Unit 8

Name _____ Date _____

Activity 2

Solve the algebra word problems. Write an equation with a variable for each problem. Draw a picture if you need to.

1. Two numbers add up to 80. The larger number is three times greater than the smaller number. What are the two numbers?

    _____

2. Two cars are traveling across the Nevada desert on the same road. They are driving toward each other. One car starts in Reno driving at 50 miles per hour. The other car starts in Las Vegas driving at 60 miles per hour. It is about 440 miles between the two cities. How long until they meet?

    _____

3. Howard, Jamal, and Michael are brothers. Howard is the youngest. Michael is the oldest. Jamal is 3 years older than Howard. Michael is 7 years older than Howard. Their combined ages are 40. How old is each brother?

    _____

Name _____ Date _____

Unit Review
Lines and Angles

Activity 1

Find the measurement of each angle in the quadrilaterals.

1. $a =$ _____

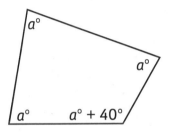

2. What are the measures of $\angle 1$, $\angle 3$, and $\angle 4$?

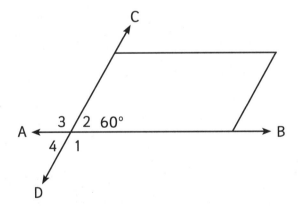

_____

What rules or properties did you use to find the angle measurements?

_____

Unit 8

Name _____ Date _____

3. What is the measure of ∠4? _____

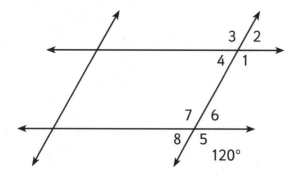

4. Find the measure of ∠12. Lines AB and CD are parallel.

∠12 = _____

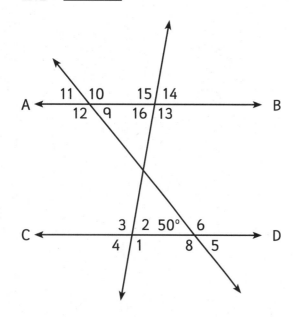

mBook Reinforce Understanding
Use the mBook *Study Guide* to review lesson concepts.

Name _____ Date _____

 Skills Maintenance
Solving Algebraic Equations

Activity 1

Evaluate the algebraic expressions.

1. Evaluate 5w if w = −5.

   _____

2. Evaluate −x + 7 if x = −2.

   _____

3. Evaluate −6z if z = 7.

   _____

4. Evaluate 3 − m if m = 12.

   _____

5. Evaluate 7n if n = −8.

   _____

Name _____ Date _____

Apply Skills
Introduction to Functions

Activity 1

Find the relationship between the two parts of each statement.

Model	Lisa gets paid $10 per hour for babysitting.
	Amount Lisa Makes ↔ Number of Hours Lisa Works
	The amount Lisa makes depends on how many hours she works.

1. Gas costs $4 per gallon.

   | Total Cost of Gas | ↔ | Number of Gallons of Gas |

   Write a statement describing the function.

   _____ depends on _____ .

2. Tina makes $8 per hour for her waitress job.

   | How Much Tina Makes | ↔ | How Many Hours Tina Works |

   Write a statement describing the function.

   _____ depends on _____ .

3. Strawberries cost $5 per pound.

   | Amount Paid for Strawberries | ↔ | Number of Pounds |

   Write a statement describing the function.

   _____ depends on _____ .

4. There is a $1 processing fee for each ticket purchased.

   | Total Processing Fees | ↔ | Number of Tickets Purchased |

   Write a statement describing the function.

   _____ depends on _____ .

Name _____ Date _____

Activity 2

Look at the function machines and tables of input and output. Complete the statement that describes each of the functions.

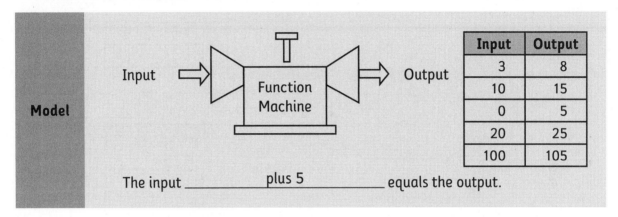

Model

Input	Output
3	8
10	15
0	5
20	25
100	105

The input _____ plus 5 _____ equals the output.

1. Input → Function Machine → Output

Input	Output
5	15
6	18
0	0
2	6
3	9

The input _____ equals the output.

Unit 9

Name _____ Date _____

2. Input 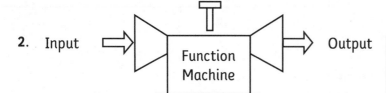 Output

Input	Output
12	5
17	10
9	2
7	0
107	100

The input _____ equals the output.

3. Input Function Machine Output

Input	Output
15	3
40	8
5	1
50	10
10	2

The input _____ equals the output.

Name _____ Date _____

 Problem-Solving Activity
Coordinate Graphs

Follow the directions to draw shapes on the graph. Make sure that each drawing uses the correct quadrants. Label the coordinates for each vertex of the shape.

Model	Draw a rectangle onto the coordinate graph. Use only Quadrants II and III.	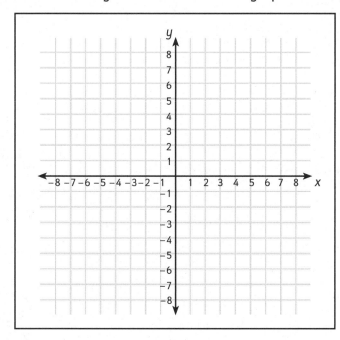

1. Draw a rectangle onto the coordinate graph. Use only Quadrants I and II.

Name _____ Date _____

2. Draw a triangle onto the coordinate graph. Use only Quadrants III and IV.

3. Draw an L shape onto the coordinate graph. Use Quadrants I, II, and IV.

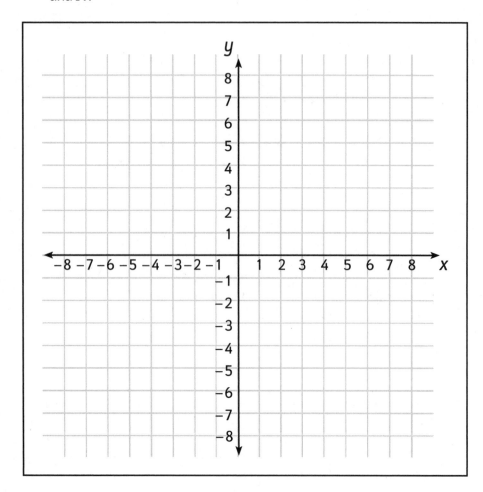

mBook **Reinforce Understanding**
Use the **mBook** *Study Guide* to review lesson concepts.

338 Unit 9 • Lesson 1

Name _____ Date _____

Skills Maintenance
Solving Algebraic Equations

Activity 1

Use mental math to solve the algebraic equations.

1. $27 = 9w$ What is the value of w? _____

2. $9 = 36 \div z$ What is the value of z? _____

3. $5y = 45$ What is the value of y? _____

4. $15 - x = 12$ What is the value of x? _____

5. $20 = 12 + a$ What is the value of a? _____

Name _____ Date _____

%÷ Apply Skills
Functions From Everyday Life

> **Activity 1**

Look at the everyday functions. Make a table of input and output that demonstrates the function. Be sure your input and output include the answer to the question that is asked. Then answer the question.

1. Suppose strawberries cost $3 per pound. How much does it cost for 5 pounds of strawberries? _____

Pounds	Cost

2. A gas station charges $4 per gallon for gas. How much does it cost for 10 gallons of gas? _____

Gallon	Cost

Name _____ Date _____

3. Elizabeth makes $10 per hour for babysitting. If Elizabeth works 6
    hours, how much does she make? _____

Hours	Payment

4. The ticket agency charges a $5 processing fee for every ticket that
    you purchase. If you buy 4 tickets, how much will you need to pay
    as a processing fee? _____

Ticket	Processing Fee

Name _____ Date _____

Problem-Solving Activity
Translations on a Coordinate Graph

Translate each shape. Each problem shows the shape in its start position. Fill out the table first, then draw the shape in its end position. Make sure you label your coordinates on the graph.

1.

Starting Points	
Vertices	**Coordinates**
A	(−8, 6)
B	(−4, 6)
C	(−8, 2)
D	(−4, 2)

Move the square a distance of 10 from Quadrant II to Quadrant I.

Ending Points	
Vertices	**Coordinates**
A'	
B'	
C'	
D'	

2.

Starting Points	
Vertices	**Coordinates**
A	(4, −1)
B	(1, −4)
C	(7, −4)

Move the triangle a distance of 5 from Quadrant IV to Quadrant I.

Ending Points	
Vertices	**Coordinates**
A'	
B'	
C'	

3.

Starting Points	
Vertices	**Coordinates**
A	(−6, 6)
B	(−4, 6)
C	(−8, 4)
D	(−2, 4)

Move the trapezoid a distance of 8 from Quadrant II to Quadrant III.

Ending Points	
Vertices	**Coordinates**
A'	
B'	
C'	
D'	

Name _____ Date _____

1.

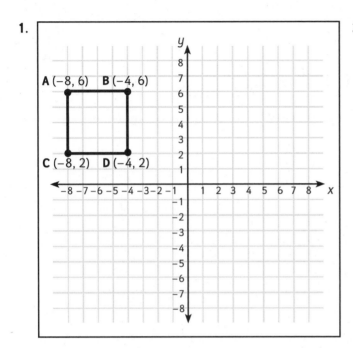

2.

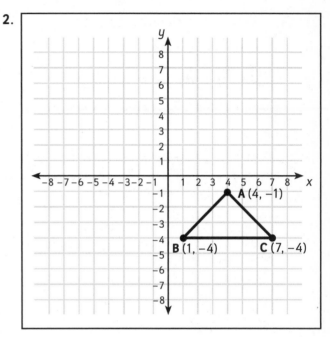

3.

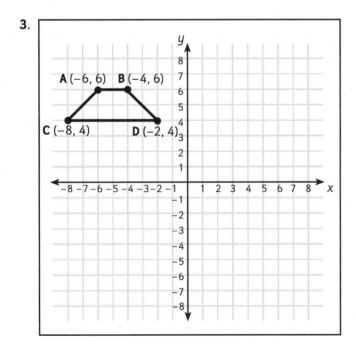

mBook **Reinforce Understanding**
Use the **mBook** *Study Guide* to review lesson concepts.

Unit 9

Name _____ Date _____

 Skills Maintenance
Coordinate Graphs

Activity 1

Plot the points on the graph. Label each point with the letter next to it.

A (3, 2) B (−1, −1) C (2, −1) D (−1, 1)

E (1, 0) F (−2, 3) G (0, 0) H (0, 1)

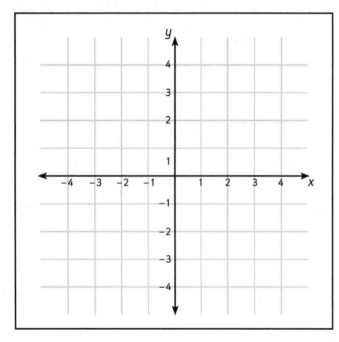

Name _____ Date _____

 Apply Skills
Graphing Functional Relationships

Activity 1

Plot each of the points from the input/output tables to make a dot graph
that represents the function. Then write a sentence that describes the
function.

1. Strawberries cost $6 per pound.

Pounds	Cost
1	$6
2	$12
3	$18
4	$24

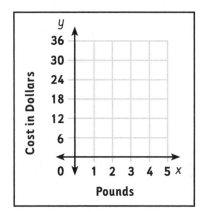

Describe the function in words.

_____

_____

2. Gas costs $4 per gallon.

Gallons	Cost
1	$4
2	$8
3	$12
4	$16

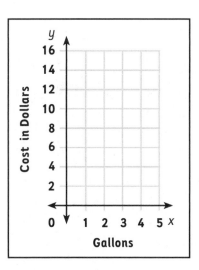

Describe the function in words.

_____

_____

Unit 9

Name _____ Date _____

Problem-Solving Activity
Reflections on a Coordinate Graph

Reflect the shapes on the coordinate graphs in each problem. Begin by using the tables and filling in the coordinates before drawing the reflected shape. Label each vertex of the reflected shape.

1.

Starting Points	
Vertices	Coordinates
A	(−4, 4)
B	(−6, 1)
C	(−2, 1)

Reflect the triangle from Quadrant II to Quadrant III.

Ending Points	
Vertices	Coordinates
A'	
B'	
C'	

2.

Starting Points	
Vertices	Coordinates
A	(−6, −1)
B	(−2, −1)
C	(−8, −3)
D	(−4, −3)

Reflect the parallelogram from Quadrant III to Quadrant IV.

Ending Points	
Vertices	Coordinates
A'	
B'	
C'	
D'	

3.

Starting Points	
Vertices	Coordinates
A	(4, −2)
B	(6, −2)
C	(2, −5)
D	(6, −5)

Reflect the trapezoid from Quadrant IV to Quadrant I.

Ending Points	
Vertices	Coordinates
A'	
B'	
C'	
D'	

Name _____ Date _____

1.

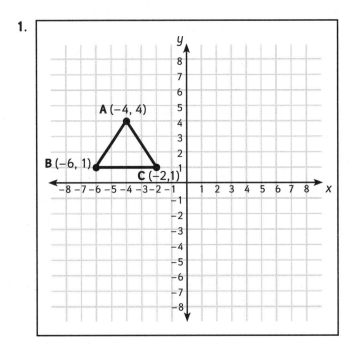

2.

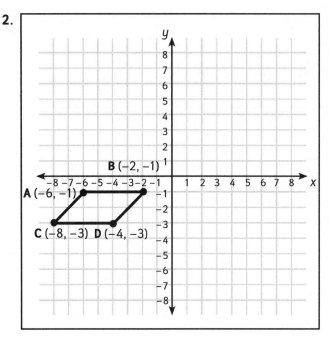

3.

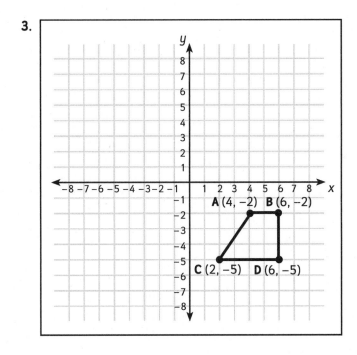

mBook Reinforce Understanding
Use the mBook *Study Guide* to review lesson concepts.

Unit 9

Name _____ Date _____

Skills Maintenance
Plotting Points

Activity 1

Plot the points on the coordinate graph. Use the letters to label the points.

A (0, 1)   B (3, 1)   C (2, −1)   D (−2, −1)

E (−1, 1)   F (0, 0)   G (−1, −2)   H (2, 0)

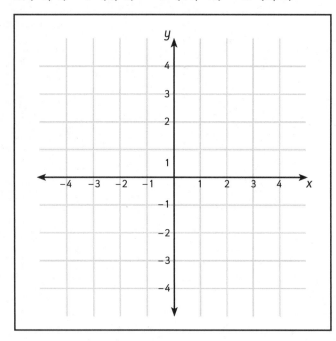

Name _____ Date _____

%÷ Apply Skills
Analyzing Functional Relationships in a Set of Data

Activity 1

Create a dot graph of the data. These data were collected from crash tests.

Speed of Car at Time of Crash	How Much the Car Length Changed as a Result of the Crash
20 mph	1 inch
40 mph	2 inches
60 mph	3 inches
80 mph	4 inches
100 mph	5 inches

The two parts of the functional relationship are:

| Speed of Car | ↔ | Change in Car Length |

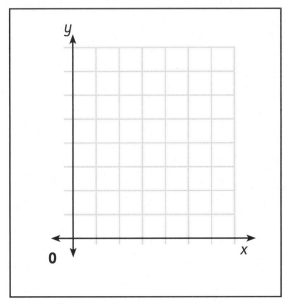

What is the relationship evident in this data?

_____

_____

_____

Name _____ Date _____

Analyze the data you collected in class that shows systematic relationship between two variables. Make a chart that shows the relationship between the functions. Then plot the functions on the blank graph. Remember to label all parts of the graph.

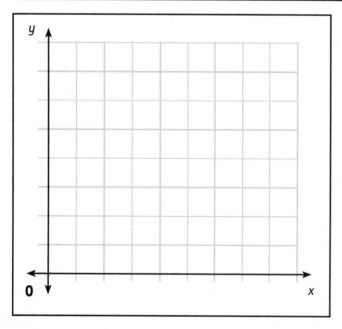

mBook **Reinforce Understanding**
Use the mBook *Study Guide* to review lesson concepts.

Name _____ Date _____

Skills Maintenance
Solving Proportions

Activity 1

Solve each of the proportions by finding the correct value for the variable.

1. $\dfrac{5}{10} = -\dfrac{10}{x}$ $x =$ _____

2. $\dfrac{1}{2} = \dfrac{w}{16}$ $w =$ _____

3. $\dfrac{z}{4} = \dfrac{15}{20}$ $z =$ _____

Substitution

Activity 2

Substitute the value of the variable and solve.

1. Solve $y = 3x$ if $x = 3$. _____

2. Solve $y = 2x$ if $x = 2$. _____

3. Solve $y = 5x$ if $x = 20$. _____

Unit 9

Name _____ Date _____

Apply Skills
The *X/Y* Table and Functions

Activity 1

Write a function for each problem using the variables *x* and *y* to describe the data in the *x/y* tables. Remember to put the *y* on the left. Check your answer by substituting in one of the *x*-values to make sure you get the corresponding *y*-value.

1. What is the function? _____

x	y
3	24
7	56
10	80
6	48
2	16

Check the answer here:

2. What is the function? _____

x	y
3	6
4	8
10	20
100	200
2	4

Check the answer here:

Name _____ Date _____

3. What is the function? _____

x	y
4	12
10	30
30	90
100	300
1	3

Check the answer here:

4. What is the function? _____

x	y
10	100
2	20
300	3,000
1	10
50	500

Check the answer here:

mBook Reinforce Understanding
Use the mBook *Study Guide* to review lesson concepts.

Name _____ Date _____

Skills Maintenance
Writing Functions

Activity 1

Write the function for each *x/y* table. Be sure to use the correct form with *y* on the left. Check your work by substituting in the values of *x* and making sure you get the correct value for *y*.

1. What is the function? _____

x	y
2	4
3	6
4	8
5	10

Check your work here:

2. What is the function? _____

x	y
1	6
2	12
3	18
4	24

Check your work here:

Name _____ Date _____

%÷ Apply Skills
Writing Functions for Everyday Situations

Activity 1

Write a function for each everyday situation. Then use the function to answer the questions about the situation.

1. Micah works at a bakery. His specialty is donuts. He bakes 12 donuts on a tray. Write a function that describes the relationship between the number of donuts and the number of trays. _____

   Questions

   (a) If Micah makes five trays of donuts, how many donuts has he baked?

   _____

   (b) How many trays would Micah need to make to get 100 donuts? _____

2. Elijah rides his bike in the evenings to prepare for a bike race. It takes him an hour to ride five miles. Write a function that describes the relationship between the number of miles and the number of hours. _____

   Questions

   (a) How far can Elijah ride in two hours?

   _____

   (b) How many miles would Elijah travel if he rode his bike for four hours?

   _____

3. Katarina gets paid $10 per hour for math tutoring. Write a function that describes how much she gets paid and how many hours she works. _____

   Questions

   (a) If Katarina earned $50 in a day, how many hours of tutoring did she do?

   _____

   (b) How much does Katarina earn if she tutors for three hours?

   _____

4. Raj makes a pitcher of iced tea each morning. He gets four 8-ounce glasses of tea from the pitcher. Write a function that describes the relationship between the number of pitchers and the number of glasses of tea. _____

   Questions

   (a) If Raj makes three pitchers of tea, how many 8-oz glasses of tea is that?

   _____

   (b) If Raj drank six glasses of tea one day, how many pitchers did he need to make that day?

   _____

Unit 9

Name _____ Date _____

Problem-Solving Activity
Graphing Linear Functions

You are given a situation and an *x/y* table in each problem. Use the data in the tables to write the functions, then draw them on the coordinate graphs.

1. Each quarter gives you time on the parking meter. The more quarters you put into the meter, the more time you get.

   Let *x* = the number of quarters and *y* = the total amount you put in the meter.

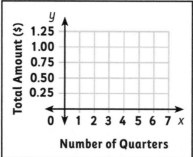

x	y
1	$0.25
2	$0.50
3	$0.75
4	$1.00
5	$1.25

2. The price of hamburger in the store is $4 per pound. Hamburger is sold in different sized packages, and what you pay depends on how much the package weighs.

   Let *x* = the number of pounds and *y* = the total cost of the hamburger.

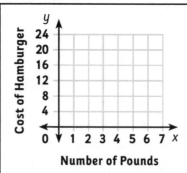

x	y
1	$4
2	$8
3	$12
4	$16
5	$20
6	$24

Name _____ Date _____

3. As gas prices get higher, people buy more small cars. Some small cars get 40 miles per gallon of gasoline. This information helps you plan how far you can drive on the number of gallons of gas in your car.

Let x = the number of gallons of gas and y = the total miles you can drive.

x	y
5	200
6	240
7	280
8	320

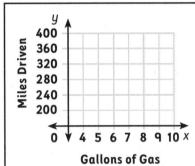

mBook **Reinforce Understanding**
Use the mBook *Study Guide* to review lesson concepts.

Unit 9 • Lesson 6   **357**

Name _____ Date _____

Skills Maintenance
Drawing Graphs of Functions

Activity 1

Use the equation and *x/y* table to graph the function. Fill in the scale on the graph to help plot the points and draw the line.

$y = 3x$ The *x/y* table is:

x	y
−1	−3
0	0
1	3
2	6
3	9

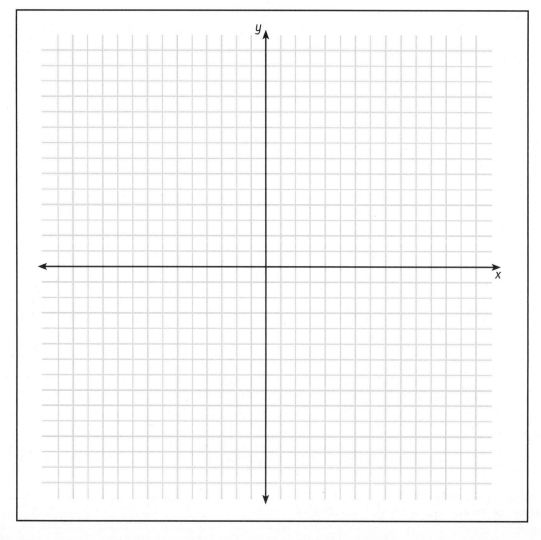

Name _____ Date _____

 Apply Skills
Slope and Linear Functions

Activity 1

Identify the slope for each of the functions.

1. $y = 3x$ The slope is _____.

2. $y = -2x$ The slope is _____.

3. $y = x$ The slope is _____.

4. $y = -\frac{2}{3}x$ The slope is _____.

Activity 2

Identify the slope of the line by looking at the rise over run on the graph.
Then write the function based on the information you see.

1.
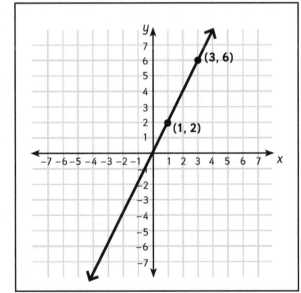

The rise is _____ and
the run is _____.

The slope is _____.

Write the function. _____

2.
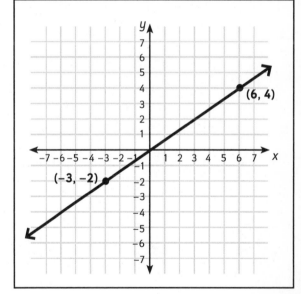

The rise is _____ and
the run is _____ .

The slope is _____.

Write the function. _____

Name _____ Date _____

3.

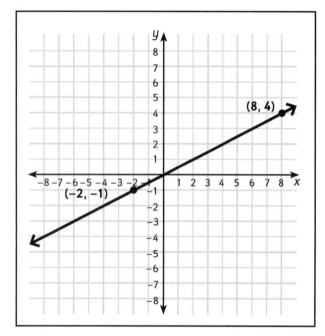

The rise is _____ and the run is _____ .

The slope is _____ . Write the function. _____

4.

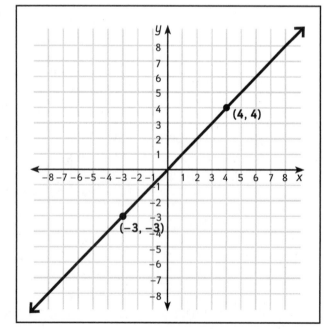

The rise is _____ and the run is _____.

The slope is _____ . Write the function. _____

Name _____ Date _____

Problem-Solving Activity
Drawing Lines

For each problem, graph a line based on the slope. Use rise over run.

1. Draw the line with the slope $\frac{1}{2}$ that goes through the point (4, 2).

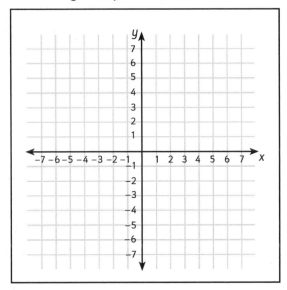

2. Draw the line with the slope −1 that goes through the point (2, −2).

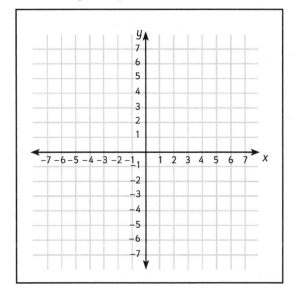

3. Draw the line with the slope 2 that goes through the point (1, 2).

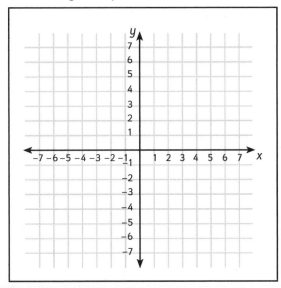

4. Draw the line with the slope $\frac{2}{3}$ that goes through the point (3, 2).

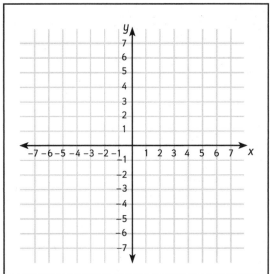

mBook Reinforce Understanding
Use the mBook *Study Guide* to review lesson concepts.

Unit 9

Name _____ Date _____

Skills Maintenance
Translations and Reflections

Activity 1

Translate or reflect the shapes and find the coordinates of the vertices of the new shape.

1. Translate the triangle 3 units up. Draw the new triangle and label the coordinates of its vertices.

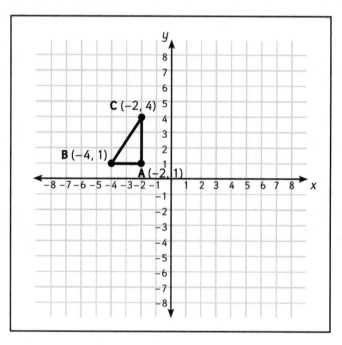

2. Reflect the square across the *x*-axis. Draw the new square and label the coordinates of its vertices.

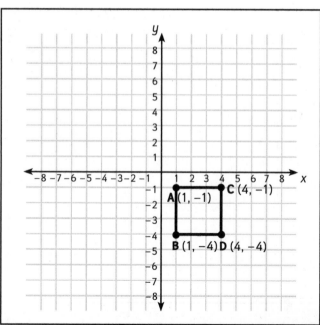

Name _____ Date _____

%÷/≥</x Apply Skills
Positive and Negative Slopes

Activity 1

Draw a line for each of the functions on the coordinate graph. Use the letters to label the lines.

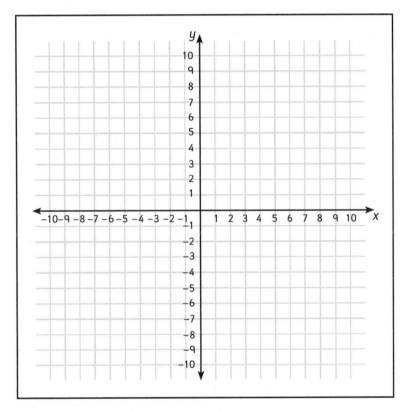

Line A: $y = 2x$ Line B: $y = -2x$ Line C: $y = 4x$ Line D: $y = -4x$

Activity 2

Write about the lines you drew in Activity 1. Tell about where the lines fall in quadrants. Describe the steepness of the lines.

_____

_____

_____

_____

_____

Name _____ Date _____

Problem-Solving Activity
Using Slopes to Analyze Functions

Select the function that matches the graph. Use your knowledge about types of slopes to help you make your decision. Then write a statement explaining how you know this is the function represented by the graph.

1. Which function is represented by this graph?

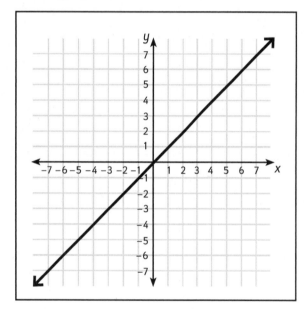

   (a) $y = -x$

   (b) $y = x$

   (c) $y = 10x$

Explain your answer.

_____

_____

_____

2. Which function is represented by this graph?

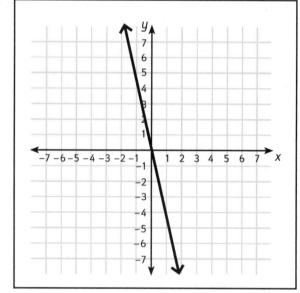

   (a) $y = -\frac{1}{2}x$

   (b) $y = 10x$

   (c) $y = -10x$

Explain your answer.

_____

_____

_____

Name _____ Date _____

3. Which function is represented by this graph?

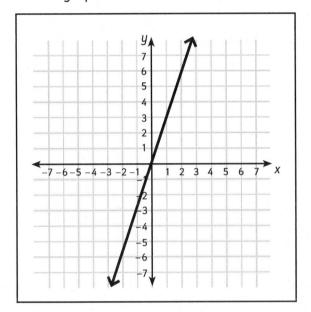

  (a) $y = -10x$

  (b) $y = x$

  (c) $y = 10x$

Explain your answer.

_____

_____

_____

4. Which function is represented by this graph?

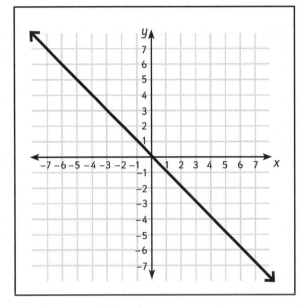

  (a) $y = -x$

  (b) $y = x$

  (c) $y = -10x$

Explain your answer.

_____

_____

_____

Name _____ Date _____

Skills Maintenance
Analyzing Slope

Activity 1

Look at the pairs of functions and think about how they look on a graph. Which of the lines is steeper? Circle the correct answer.

1. Line A: $y = 2x$

    Line B: $y = 3x$

    Which line has the steeper slope? (circle one)   A   or   B

2. Line A: $y = -2x$

    Line B: $y = -3x$

    Which line has the steeper slope? (circle one)   A   or   B

3. Line A: $y = \frac{1}{2}x$

    Line B: $y = 3x$

    Which line has the steeper slope? (circle one)   A   or   B

Activity 2

Tell which quadrants the line appears in on a coordinate graph. Circle the correct answer.

1. Where is the line $y = -x$?

    (circle one)   Quadrants II & IV   or   Quadrants I & III

2. Where is the line $y = \frac{1}{2}x$?

    (circle one)   Quadrants II & IV   or   Quadrants I & III

3. Where is the line $y = -\frac{3}{4}x$?

    (circle one)   Quadrants II & IV   or   Quadrants I & III

Name _____ Date _____

⅗ Apply Skills
Rate of Change

Activity 1

Tell who reached their goal first by completing the *x/y* tables and graphing the functions.

1. The goal is to score 60 points. Marcus scores 15 points per level and Liza scores 20 points per level.

   Complete the *x/y* tables. The *x* stands for level and the *y* stands for points.

Marcus's Points		Liza's Points	
x	y	x	y
1	15	1	20
2		2	
3		3	

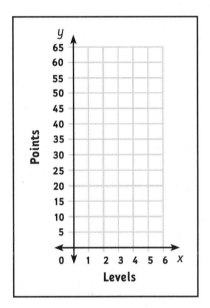

   Graph the functions. Who reached the goal first? _____

2. The goal is to make $30 babysitting. Hannah makes $6 per hour and Ali makes $5 per hour.

   Complete the *x/y* tables. The *x* stands for hours and the *y* stands for earnings.

Hannah's Earnings		Ali's Earnings	
x	y	x	y
1	6	1	5
2		2	
3		3	
4		4	
5		5	
6		6	

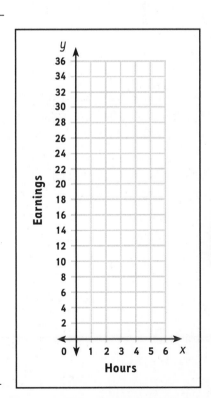

   Graph the functions. Who reached the goal first? _____

Name _____ Date _____

Problem-Solving Activity
The Advantage of Lines

In each of the problems, interpret the graph based on two functions. Use what you know about coordinate graphs to answer the questions.

1. Janelle and her sister Tanya are leaving their house in two different cars. They are both driving on the same road, and they are going on a long trip. Janelle is driving at 40 miles per hour and Tanya is driving at 50 miles per hour. How much farther ahead will Tanya be after 4 hours? What about after 6 hours?

    _____

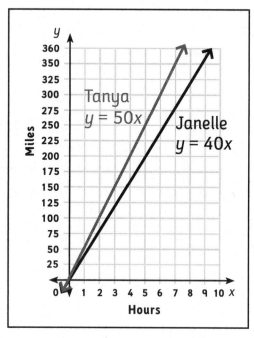

2. Satellites move around the Earth in space. They travel at different speeds. Some are faster than others. At noon a TV satellite and a spy satellite are next to each other in space. The spy satellite is going 80 miles per minute and the TV satellite is going 60 miles per minute. How much farther will the spy satellite be after 8 minutes? What about after 12 minutes?

    _____

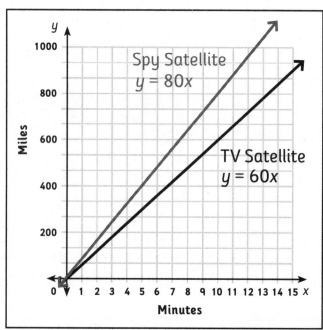

Name _____ Date _____

3. Two gears are part of a large machine that makes dog food. If the gears didn't turn, there would be no dog food. Gear A makes 5 turns a minute and Gear B makes 7 turns a minute. When you turn on the machine, the gears are in the same starting place. How many more turns will Gear B make after 4 minutes? What about 8 minutes?

_____

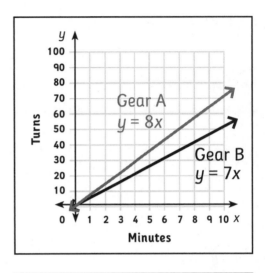

4. Two other machines in the factory pour the dog food into sacks and seal each one of them. They're ready to be put in boxes after that. The large machine pours and seals 15 sacks per minute. The small machine pours and seals 10 sacks per minute. How many more sacks will the large machine pour and seal after 3 minutes? What about after 8 minutes?

_____

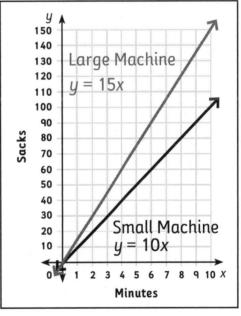

mBook Reinforce Understanding
Use the mBook *Study Guide* to review lesson concepts.

Unit 9

Name _____ Date _____

Skills Maintenance
Solving Equations With Variables

Activity 1

Solve the equations by substituting the value for the variable.

1. Solve $y = 2x + 1$ if $x = 2$. _____

2. Solve $y = -x + 5$ if $x = -3$. _____

3. Solve $y = x + 7$ if $x = 10$. _____

4. Solve $y = \frac{1}{2} x + 10$ if $x = 6$. _____

Name _____ Date _____

Apply Skills
The Y-Intercept

Activity 1

Find the functions for each problem. Each problem describes a situation and provides a table of data. Your job is to:

(a) Label the *x*- and *y*-axes based on the information in the problem.

(b) Draw the line on the graph.

(c) Write the function.

1. Watch It Tonight! is a local video store that rents movies. They have a plan where you pay $10 per month, and then $2 per movie. This way you can watch as many movies as you want for the month for just $2 each. The table shows the total cost to rent movies (up to 5).

Number of Movies	Cost for Videos	Monthly Charge	Total Cost
0	0	10	10
1	2	10	12
2	4	10	14
3	6	10	16
4	8	10	18
5	10	10	20

Write the function. _____

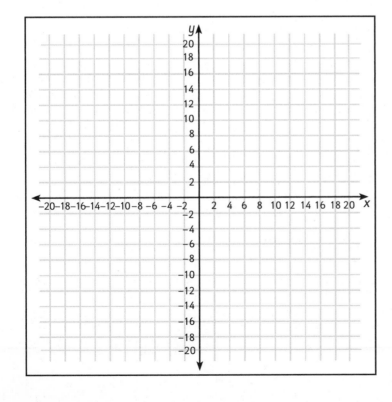

Name _____ Date _____

2. Watch It Tonight! decided that it was not getting enough business by charging $10 per month, so it dropped its monthly charge to $7 per month. Here is a new table that shows the cost of renting up to five videos per month.

Number of Movies	Cost for Videos	Monthly Charge	Total Cost
0	0	7	7
1	2	7	9
2	4	7	11
3	6	7	13
4	8	7	15
5	10	7	17

Write the function. _____

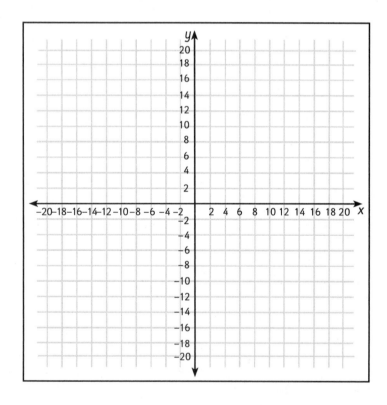

mBook Reinforce Understanding
Use the mBook *Study Guide* to review lesson concepts.

Name _____ Date _____

 Skills Maintenance
Solving Equations With Variables

Activity 1

Solve the equations by substituting the value for the variable.

1. Solve $y = 2x + 3$ for $x = -1$. _____

2. Solve $y = 3x - 1$ for $x = -2$. _____

3. Solve $y = 2x + 5$ for $x = 1$. _____

4. Solve $y = \frac{1}{2}x + 10$ for $x = 8$. _____

Name _____ Date _____

%÷ **Apply Skills**
<=x **Slope Intercept Form:** $y = mx + b$

Activity 1

Fill in the *x/y* table and make a graph for each of the functions written in slope-intercept form.

1. Function: $y = 2x + 2$

x	y

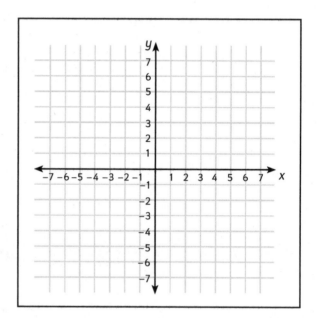

Draw the graph.

What is the slope? _____

What is the *y*-intercept? _____

2. Function: $y = x - 2$

x	y

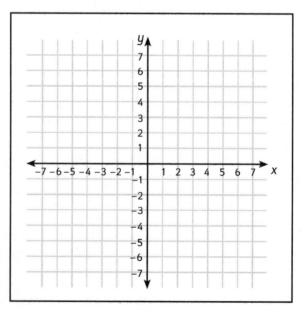

Draw the graph.

What is the slope? _____

What is the *y*-intercept? _____

Name _____ Date _____

3. Function: $y = \frac{1}{2}x + -1$

x	y

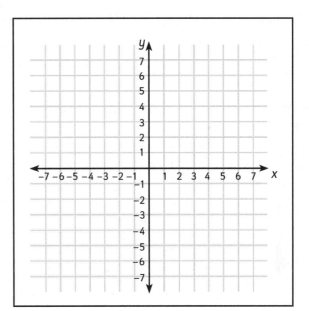

Draw the graph.

What is the slope? _____

What is the y-intercept? _____

Name _____ Date _____

Problem-Solving Activity
Graphing Linear Equations

You learned about three kinds of slopes:
- Positive slope
- Negative slope
- Zero slope

Match the functions with the graphs in each problem. Think about the direction of the line and rise-over-run when you figure out which function goes with what graph.

Functions:

$y = -2x + 3$ $y = 4x - 1$ $y = 0x + 3$ $y = -4x + 1$ $y = 0x - 1$

1. Which function goes with this graph?

2. Which function goes with this graph?

_____

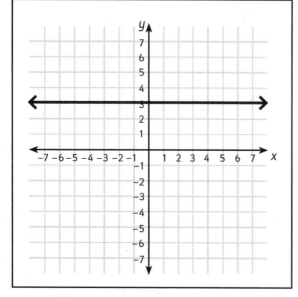

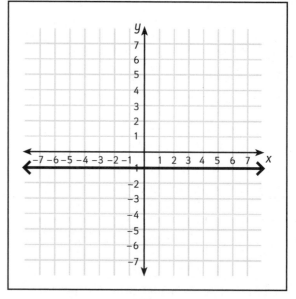

Explain the feature of the graph that helped you make this choice.

_____

_____

_____

Explain the feature of the graph that helped you make this choice.

_____

_____

_____

Name _____ Date _____

3. Which function goes with this graph?

_____

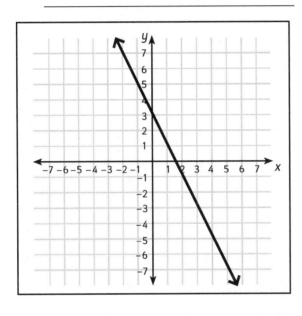

Explain the feature of the graph that helped you make this choice.

_____

_____

_____

4. Which function goes with this graph?

_____

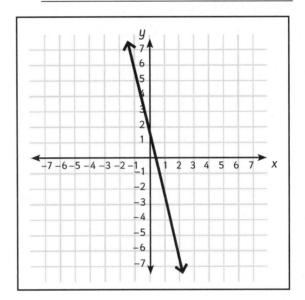

Explain the feature of the graph that helped you make this choice.

_____

_____

_____

5. Which function goes with this graph?

_____

Explain the feature of the graph that helped you make this choice.

_____

_____

_____

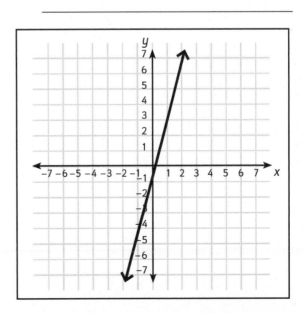

Unit 9

Name _____ Date _____

 Skills Maintenance
y = mx + b

Activity 1

Use the form *y = mx + b* to write a function for each problem. Remember, *m* is the slope and *b* is the *y*-intercept.

1. Write the equation for the function where the slope is −2 and the *y*-intercept is 5.

   _____

2. Write the equation for the function where the slope is −1 and the *y*-intercept is 0.

   _____

3. Write the equation for the function where the slope is 1 and the *y*-intercept is 1.

   _____

4. Write the equation for the function where the slope is 0 and the *y*-intercept is 2.

   _____

Name _____ Date _____

%÷ Apply Skills
Algebraic Equations and Functions

> **Activity 1**

Suppose you rent a car from Dented Rentals. The base charge is $20, plus 25 cents per mile. The equation for this function looks like this: $y = 0.25x + 20$. Each problem gives you a total charge amount for different scenarios. Find the amount of miles you have to drive to reach each amount.

1. The total amount you owe Dented Rentals is $140. Here is the equation: $140 = 0.25x + 20$. How many miles did you travel?

   _____

   Show your work here:

2. The total amount you owe Dented Rentals is $200. Here is the equation: $200 = 0.25x + 20$. How many miles did you travel?

   _____

   Show your work here:

3. The total amount you owe Dented Rentals is $380. Here is the equation: $380 = 0.25x + 20$. How many miles did you travel?

   _____

   Show your work here:

Name _____ Date _____

 Problem-Solving Activity
More Graphs of Linear Functions

Write the word problems in $y = mx + b$ form, then solve algebraically.
Remember the four steps for solving these kinds of problems:
Step 1: Decide what is changing and what is staying the same.
Step 2: Find what each variable represents in the function.
Step 3: Substitute numbers for the variables in the function.
Step 4: Solve the equation.

1. Juliana sells programs at baseball games. She makes $5 per night
    and $2 for every program she sells. At the end of Thursday night,
    she made $37. How many programs did she sell?

    _____

2. A carpet cleaning service charges a base fee of $10 to clean
    carpets, then $2 for every square yard. The bill to clean the house
    was $58. How many square yards did the service clean?

    _____

3. A wagon is used to move boxes around the warehouse. The wagon
    weighs 40 pounds and each box weighs 5 pounds. After Cesar
    stacked the wagon with boxes, the wagon and the boxes weighed
    95 pounds. How many boxes did Cesar stack on the wagon?

    _____

mBook **Reinforce Understanding**
Use the mBook *Study Guide* to review lesson concepts.

Name _____ Date _____

Skills Maintenance
Identifying Coordinates on a Graph

Activity 1

Write the coordinates for each point on the graph.

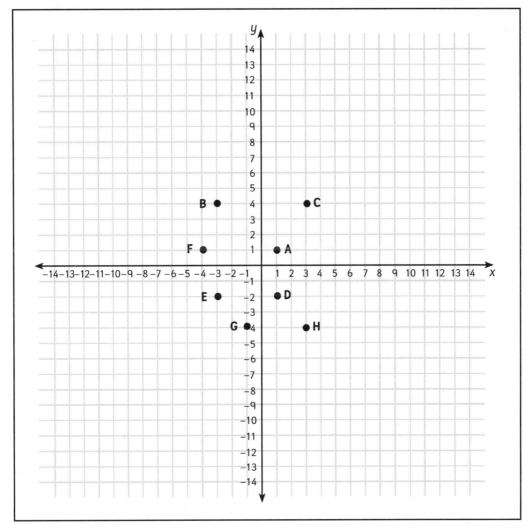

Write the coordinates.

A _____ B _____ C _____ D _____

E _____ F _____ G _____ H _____

Name _____ Date _____

%÷ Apply Skills
Creating an *X/Y* Table From a Graph

Activity 1

Create an *x/y* table for each problem. Then tell the function in
y = *mx* + *b* form.

1.

x	y

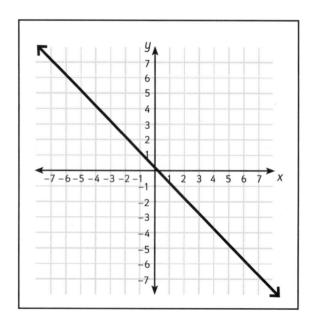

2.

x	y

Name _____ Date _____

Problem-Solving Activity
The Point Where Functions Intersect on a Graph

Write two functions to solve each problem. Use algebra to find where the two functions cross on the graph. Then plot the functions on a graph to see where they intersect.

1. Garrison Motors has two plans for buying new cars.

    Plan 1: You pay $450 per month.

    Plan 2: You pay $1,000 down and pay $250 per month.

    What are the two functions?

    _____

    How many months before you pay the same amount with both plans?

    _____

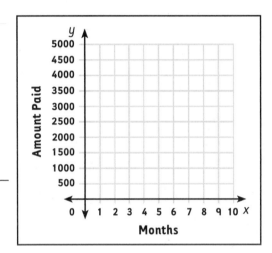

2. Raul is getting a summer job delivering pizza. He has done it before, and he has to choose between two different companies. Bonzo Pizza will pay him $10 a day and $3 for every pizza he delivers. Too Hot to Eat Pizza will pay him $5 for every pizza he delivers.

    What are the two functions?

    _____

    At what point will he make the same amount of money?

    _____

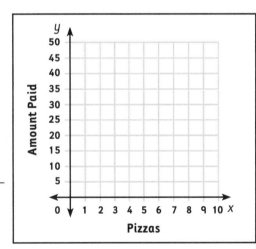

Unit 9

Name _____ Date _____

Skills Maintenance
Finding the Intersecting Points

Activity 1

Look at the graphs. Write the coordinates of the point where the two functions meet.

1.

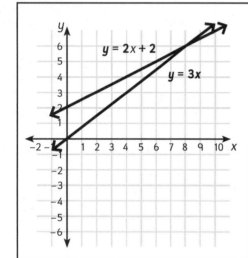

The two lines intersect at the point _____.

2.

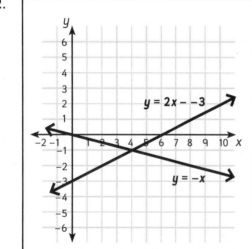

The two lines intersect at the point _____.

Name _____ Date _____

%÷ **Apply Skills**
Creating an Equation From a Graph

Activity 1

Look at each of the graphs. Analyze the line and find the slope,
y-intercept, and equation in $y = mx + b$ form.

1.

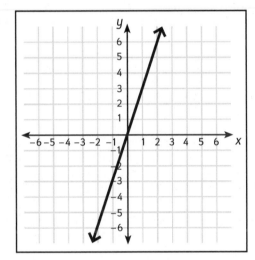

What is the slope? _____

What is the y-intercept? _____

What is the equation? _____

2.

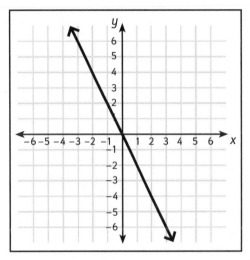

What is the slope? _____

What is the y-intercept? _____

What is the equation? _____

3.

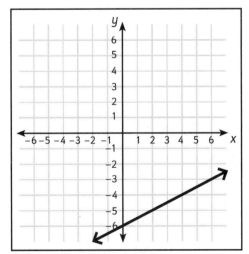

What is the slope? _____

What is the y-intercept? _____

What is the equation? _____

4.

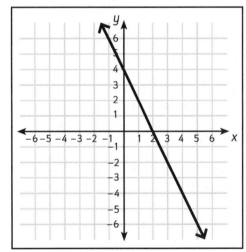

What is the slope? _____

What is the y-intercept? _____

What is the equation? _____

Unit 9

Name _____ Date _____

Problem-Solving Activity
Using a Function to Find the Best Deal

Find the job or activity that is the best deal. Write functions from each of the word problems, then plot them on the graph.

1. Mindy has the choice of two different jobs at Thompson's Manufacturing. She wants the job that will pay her the most money per week. Her choices are:

   a. Work as a receptionist answering phones. She gets a base pay of $50 per week and $8 per hour.

   b. Work in shipping packing boxes. She gets a base pay of $10 per hour.

   Mindy can only work 40 hours per week. At what point will she make the same amount for both jobs? Which job should she take if she wants to make the most money per week?

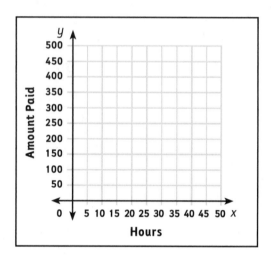

_____

2. Rachel volunteered to walk on Sunday for people with cancer. She wants to raise as much money as she can. She has to choose between two ways to raise money.

   a. She gets $20 just to do the walk and $2 for every mile she walks.

   b. She gets $3 for every mile she walks.

   How far does Rachel have to walk before she raises the same amount of money?

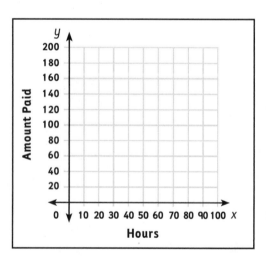

_____

Let's say Rachel can walk 15 miles. Which plan should she choose in order to raise the most money?

_____

Name _____   Date _____

Skills Maintenance
Substitution

| Activity 1 |

Substitute the value of the variable and solve.

1. Solve $y = 3x$ if $x = 5$. _____

2. Solve $y = 2x$ if $x = 1$. _____

3. Solve $y = 5x$ if $x = 5$. _____

4. Solve $y = x + 4$ if $x = 1$. _____

5. Solve $y = 7x + 23$ if $x = 7$. _____

6. Solve $y = -3x + 5$ if $x = 4$. _____

7. Solve $y = 4x - 10$ if $x = -2$. _____

8. Solve $y = -9x - 10$ if $x = -3$. _____

Name _____ Date _____

Unit Review
Introduction to Functions

Activity 1

Write a function based on each table of data.

1.

x	y
9	27
2	6
5	15
4	12

Function _____

2.

x	y
−3	3
4	10
−10	−4
2	8

Function _____

Activity 2

Write a function for each word problem.

1. The water bill for your house depends on how much water you use. You probably use a lot more in the summer. The water company has a basic charge of $20 per month plus $3 for every hundred gallons that you use. _____

2. Campino's Go-Cart Track is a place for serious go-cart drivers. If you want to drive a lot, Campino has a special rate. It's $10 a week plus $3 a race. You can race as many times as you want during the week. Leo loves go-carts and spent $43 last week at Campino's. How many races was she in? _____

Name _____ Date _____

 Unit Review
Working With Coordinate Graphs

Activity 1

Create an *x/y* table based on the function. Then plot the function on the coordinate graph.

$y = 2x - 3$

x	y

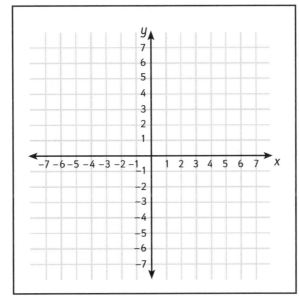

Draw the lines for this function on the coordinate graph: $y = \frac{1}{2}x + 4$.

Where do the two lines meet? _____

Activity 2

Answer the questions about each function.

1. Which line is steeper?

   (a) $y = 2x + 3$

   (b) $y = \frac{1}{2}x + 3$

   (c) $y = 3x + 2$

   (d) $y = x + 5$

2. Which line is steeper?

   (a) $y = 4x$

   (b) $y = \frac{3}{4}x$

   (c) $y = x + 6$

   (d) $y = \frac{1}{2}x + 10$

Name _____ Date _____

Activity 3

Use algebra to answer the questions. Decide which scenario will give you the best deal. Then graph the functions for each problem on a coordinate graph and label the point where they intersect.

1. Your family decides it needs new carpet in the entire house. You can pay for the carpet and the work to install it in two ways:

    a: Pay $50 per month.

    b: Pay $100 down and $25 per month.

    When will you pay the same amount?

    _____

    What plan is the better deal?

    _____

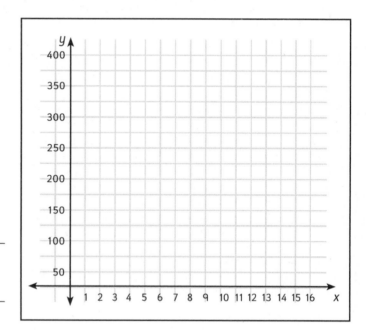

2. You want to make as much money as you can in your summer job. You have two jobs to choose from. Each job will pay you by the week.

    a: You can work on the factory floor for $10 an hour.

    b: You can work on the night shift cleaning floors. You make $30 per week as a base pay and $8 per hour.

    When will you make the same amount of money?

    _____

    Which job should you take?

    _____

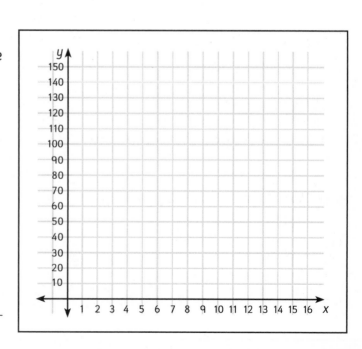

Name _____ Date _____

 Skills Maintenance
Substitution

Activity 1

Solve the equations by using substitution.

1. Solve $y = 3x + 2$ if $x = 8$. _____

2. Solve $y = -x - 3$ if $x = 6$. _____

3. Solve $y = 2x - 4$ if $x = 5$. _____

4. Solve $y = -4x + -12$ if $x = 7$. _____

Name _____ Date _____

%÷/= <x Apply Skills
The Pythagorean Theorem

Activity 1

Find the areas of the shapes by substituting the dimensions into the area formulas.

1. Area of a Rectangle = base • height

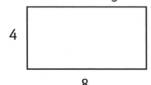

4

8

What is the area of the rectangle?

_____ square units

2. Area of a Square = base • height

5

5

What is the area of the square?

_____ square units

3. Area of a Triangle = $\frac{1}{2}$ (base • height)

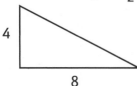

4

8

What is the area of the triangle?

_____ square units

Activity 2

Match the type of triangle with its picture.

1. △ _____   **(a)** Scalene

2. ◁ _____   **(b)** Right

3. ◣ _____   **(c)** Isosceles

4. ◿ _____   **(d)** Equilateral

Name _____ Date _____

Activity 3

Prove that the Pythagorean Theorem works using the area of squares. We will change the area formula for squares slightly. You can see that both formulas give you the same area. Look at the model then at the triangle and squares. Then answer the questions about the sides of the triangle.

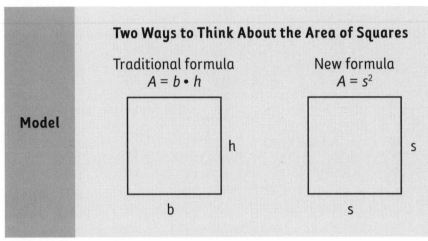

Model

Two Ways to Think About the Area of Squares

Traditional formula
$A = b \cdot h$

New formula
$A = s^2$

h

b

s

s

We can show that the Pythagorean Theorem works by drawing squares onto each side of a right triangle as shown. Think about how the area of those squares helps prove the Pythagorean Theorem.

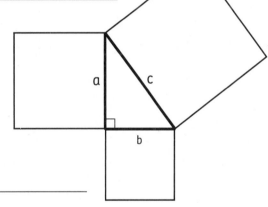

a   c

b

1. What do we know about each of the sides of the right triangle based on the three squares?

   _____

2. What do squared units have to do with the Pythagorean Theorem?

   _____

   _____

3. If the measurements of the sides of a right triangle are as follows: $a = 3$, $b = 4$, and $c = 5$, does this demonstrate that the Pythagorean Theorem works?

   _____

Name _____ Date _____

4. Draw three squares forming a right triangle in the middle of the graph. Use the dimensions of the squares you drew as your lengths a, b, and c. Test the Pythagorean Theorem using this data.

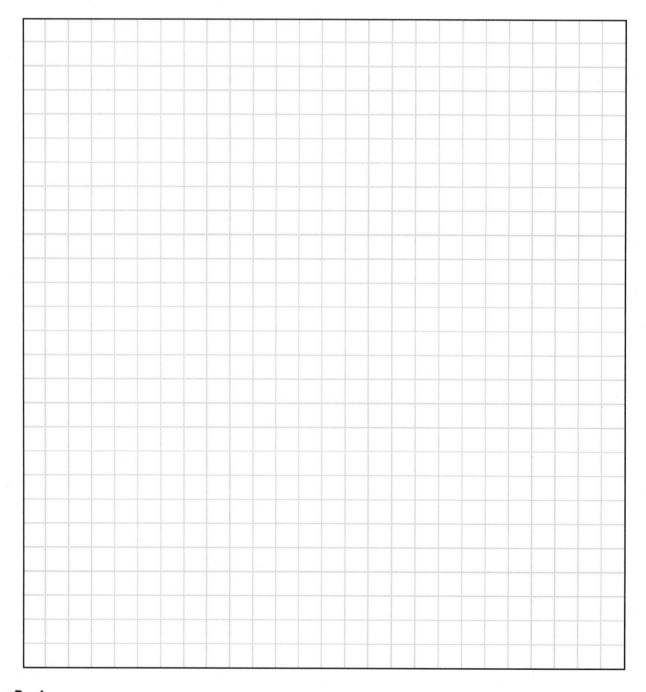

mBook **Reinforce Understanding**
Use the mBook *Study Guide* to review lesson concepts.

Name _____ Date _____

 Skills Maintenance
Square Numbers

Activity 1

Write each number as repeated multiplication, then find its
square number.

Model	$5^2 = \underline{5} \cdot \underline{5} = \underline{25}$

1. 2^2 = _____ • _____ = _____

2. 4^2 = _____ • _____ = _____

3. 7^2 = _____ • _____ = _____

4. 10^2 = _____ • _____ = _____

5. 3^2 = _____ • _____ = _____

Name _____ Date _____

Apply Skills
Square Numbers and Square Roots

> ### Activity 1

Find the square root of each number. Remember to include negative numbers. Round decimal numbers to the nearest hundredth.

Model	$\sqrt{100}$ +10 or −10

1. $\sqrt{49}$ _____ or _____

2. $\sqrt{64}$ _____ or _____

3. $\sqrt{16}$ _____ or _____

4. $\sqrt{1}$ _____ or _____

5. $\sqrt{63}$ _____ or _____

6. $\sqrt{81}$ _____ or _____

7. $\sqrt{121}$ _____ or _____

8. $\sqrt{14}$ _____ or _____

> ### Activity 2

Find the square roots of sides for different shapes. Be sure to remember these two formulas:

Area of a square

$A = s^2$

Pythagorean Theorem

$a^2 + b^2 = c^2$

Do not use a calculator in this exercise. Remember what you know about numbers and square numbers. For example, if you see a number like 25, you know that it is the same as 5 · 5. That means the square root of 25 is 5. If the number is not one that you know well, just write the square root symbol.

Name _____ Date _____

1. What is the length of side *a*? _____

Area of the square = 100

a

2. What is the length of side *c*? _____

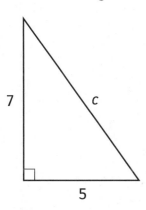

7   *c*

5

3. What is the length of side *d*? _____

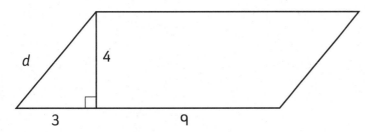

d   4

3   9

Name _____ Date _____

4. What is the length of side *r*? _____

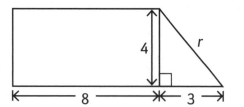

5. What is the length of side *m*? _____

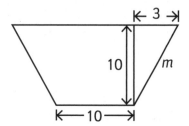

6. What is the length of side *b*? _____

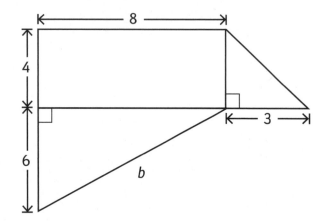

mBook **Reinforce Understanding**
Use the mBook *Study Guide* to review lesson concepts.

398 Unit 10 • Lesson 2

Name _____ Date _____

 Skills Maintenance
Square Roots

Activity 1

Find the square root of each number. Use a calculator to find the answers
to numbers that are not perfect squares. Round decimal numbers to the
nearest hundred-thousandth.

Model

$\sqrt{17}$ _____ or _____
Using a calculator, you get this answer.

4.1231056256176605

Round your answer.
$\sqrt{17}$ ____4.12311____ or ____−4.12311____

1. $\sqrt{144}$ _____ or _____

2. $\sqrt{145}$ _____ or _____

3. $\sqrt{5}$ _____ or _____

4. $\sqrt{4}$ _____ or _____

5. $\sqrt{10}$ _____ or _____

6. $\sqrt{9}$ _____ or _____

7. $\sqrt{196}$ _____ or _____

Name _____ Date _____

 Apply Skills
Applying the Pythagorean Theorem

Activity 1

Use the Pythagorean theorem to find the missing lengths of the sides of right triangles. You may need to find the length of side *a*, *b*, or *c*. If your answer is not a perfect square, leave the square root as your answer.

1. What is the length of side *a*? _____

   Show your work here.

   $a^2 + b^2 = c^2$

   $a = ?$ $c = 5$ $b = 4$

2. What is the length of side *b*? _____

   Show your work here.

   $a^2 + b^2 = c^2$

   $b = ?$ $a = 8$ $c = 9$

3. What is the length of side *c*? _____

   Show your work here.

   $a^2 + b^2 = c^2$

   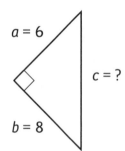

   $a = 6$ $c = ?$ $b = 8$

Name _____ Date _____

4. What is the length of side *a*? _____
    Show your work here.
    $a^2 + b^2 = c^2$

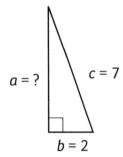

5. What is the length of side *b*? _____
    Show your work here.
    $a^2 + b^2 = c^2$

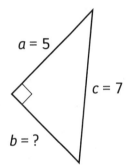

6. What is the length of side *c*? _____
    Show your work here.
    $a^2 + b^2 = c^2$

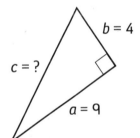

Name _____ Date _____

Activity 2

Use what you know about the Pythagorean Theorem to solve the problems. Round decimal numbers to the nearest tenth. Think about why the distance is important for each sport.

1. In football, teams can score points by kicking a field goal. When a player kicks a field goal, it is a lot easier (and shorter) if he is straight in front of the goal post. How far is it if he kicks the field goal from near the sidelines?

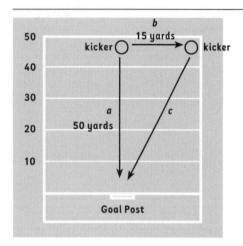

2. A quarterback doesn't have to throw the ball as far from the middle of the field than from the sideline. A longer throw means there is more a chance the ball will be intercepted by the other team. How far does the quarterback throw the ball from the sidelines?

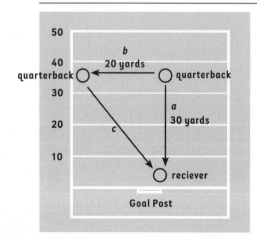

Name _____ Date _____

3. A basketball player shoots a three-point shot straight at the basket. This is a distance of about 20 feet. If the player moves 15 feet to the right, it is a much longer shot. How far is the longer shot?

_____

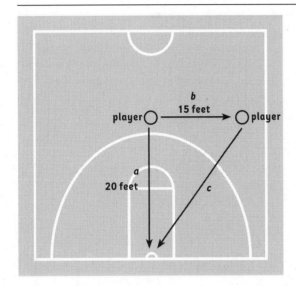

4. A golfer does not have to hit the ball as far is she is in front of the pin on the green. If she is off to the side, the shot is farther. How far is it to hit the shot from the side?

_____

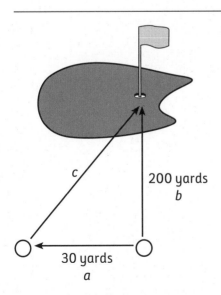

mBook Reinforce Understanding
Use the **mBook** *Study Guide* to review lesson concepts.

Unit 10

Name _____ Date _____

Skills Maintenance
Using the Pythagorean Theorem

Activity 1

Use the Pythagorean theorem to find the length of the missing side for each right triangle. Round decimal numbers to the nearest tenth.

1. What is the length of side a? _____

Show your work here.

$a^2 + b^2 = c^2$

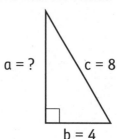

$a = ?$ $c = 8$

$b = 4$

2. What is the length of side b? _____

Show your work here.

$a^2 + b^2 = c^2$

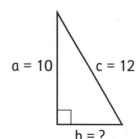

$a = 10$ $c = 12$

$b = ?$

3. What is the length of side c? _____

Show your work here.

$a^2 + b^2 = c^2$

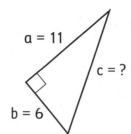

$a = 11$

$c = ?$

$b = 6$

Name _____ Date _____

Problem-Solving Activity
Non-Linear Functions

Create x/y tables for each of the non-linear functions. You may use a calculator.

1. $y = x^2 + 1$

x	y

2. $y = x^3$

x	y

3. $y = x^4$

x	y

4. $y = x^2 - 1$

x	y

5. $y = x^3 - 1$

x	y

Name _____ Date _____

Problem-Solving Activity
Non-Linear Functions

Create a table and graph for the function $y = x^2$. Notice that the x/y table includes negative values for x. The graph you are making will result in a line that is not straight. Once you finish the graph, explain why the line curves up in Quadrant II. Use information from the function and the table to explain why the function is U-shaped.

$y = x^2$

x	y
−3	
−2	
−1	
0	
1	
2	
3	

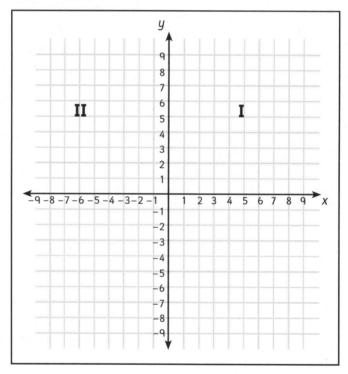

1. What do you notice about the y-values for the x-values −3 and 3?

   _____

   _____

2. Explain in your own words why the graph of this function is curved.

   _____

   _____

   _____

mBook **Reinforce Understanding**
Use the **mBook** *Study Guide* to review lesson concepts.

Name _____ Date _____

 Skills Maintenance
Finding Square Roots

Activity 1

Find the square root of each number. Use a calculator to find the numbers that are not perfect squares. Round to the nearest hundredth. Don't forget to include the negative numbers.

1. $\sqrt{49}$ _____ or _____

2. $\sqrt{50}$ _____ or _____

3. $\sqrt{64}$ _____ or _____

4. $\sqrt{65}$ _____ or _____

5. $\sqrt{74}$ _____ or _____

6. $\sqrt{81}$ _____ or _____

Name _____ Date _____

%÷ Apply Skills
Properties of Irrational Numbers

Activity 1

Circle the numbers that are irrational numbers in the list. Then explain how you can tell irrational numbers from rational numbers.

$$\sqrt{13} \quad 4.2 \quad \sqrt{4} \quad -3 \quad -\frac{1}{4} \quad 5 \quad \sqrt{5} \quad -2.1 \quad \frac{2}{3}$$

How can you tell irrational numbers from rational numbers?

_____

_____

_____

_____

Activity 2

Find the square roots of each number. You may use a calculator. Round the irrational numbers to the nearest tenth. Remember to include the negative numbers.

Number	Square Roots	Number	Square Roots
$\sqrt{9}$	_____ and _____	$\sqrt{10}$	_____ and _____
$\sqrt{11}$	_____ and _____	$\sqrt{13}$	_____ and _____
$\sqrt{16}$	_____ and _____	$\sqrt{20}$	_____ and _____
$\sqrt{25}$	_____ and _____	$\sqrt{27}$	_____ and _____
$\sqrt{30}$	_____ and _____	$\sqrt{33}$	_____ and _____
$\sqrt{36}$	_____ and _____	$\sqrt{40}$	_____ and _____
$\sqrt{45}$	_____ and _____	$\sqrt{49}$	_____ and _____
$\sqrt{50}$	_____ and _____	$\sqrt{55}$	_____ and _____
$\sqrt{64}$	_____ and _____	$\sqrt{69}$	_____ and _____

mBook Reinforce Understanding
Use the mBook *Study Guide* to review lesson concepts.

Name _____ Date _____

Skills Maintenance
Finding Square Roots

Activity 1

Solve the square roots. Use your calculator to find the numbers that are
not perfect squares. Round your answers to the nearest tenth. Remember
to include the negative numbers.

1. $\sqrt{89}$ _____ and _____

2. $\sqrt{95}$ _____ and _____

3. $\sqrt{100}$ _____ and _____

4. $\sqrt{112}$ _____ and _____

5. $\sqrt{121}$ _____ and _____

6. $\sqrt{136}$ _____ and _____

7. $\sqrt{141}$ _____ and _____

8. $\sqrt{144}$ _____ and _____

Name _____ Date _____

 Problem-Solving Activity
The Direction of Non-Linear Functions

Create an *x/y* table for each of the functions. Remember to use the rules from PEMDAS. Solve the exponent before you multiply by the coefficient.

1. $y = \frac{1}{2}x^2$

x	y
−2	
−1	
0	
1	
2	

2. $y = -x^2$

x	y
−2	
−1	
0	
1	
2	

3. $y = -2x^2$

x	y
−2	
−1	
0	
1	
2	

4. $y = -2x^2 + 1$

x	y
−2	
−1	
0	
1	
2	

Name _____ Date _____

Problem-Solving Activity
The Direction of Non-Linear Functions

Create a table and graph for the functions $y = x^2$ and $y = -x^2$. After you create them, answer the questions about the two functions.

$y = x^2$

x	y
−3	
−2	
−1	
0	
1	
2	
3	

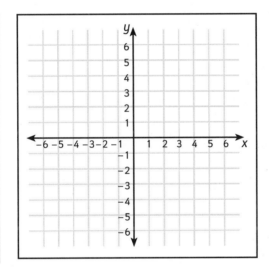

$y = -x^2$

x	y
−3	
−2	
−1	
0	
1	
2	
3	

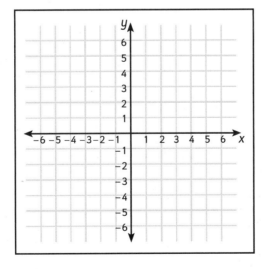

Name _____ Date _____

1. How do the tables differ for the two functions? Give examples.

   _____

   _____

   _____

   _____

   _____

2. How do the graphs differ for the two functions? Give examples.

   _____

   _____

   _____

   _____

   _____

3. Explain how the coefficient affects the tables and graphs of the functions.

   _____

   _____

   _____

   _____

   _____

mBook Reinforce Understanding
Use the mBook *Study Guide* to review lesson concepts.

Name _____ Date _____

Skills Maintenance
Nonlinear Functions

Activity 1

Create *x/y* tables for the nonlinear functions. Remember to use **PEMDAS** and solve the exponent first. The *x*-values are filled in for you.

1. $y = -2x^2$

x	y
−2	
−1	
0	
1	
2	

2. $y = 5x^2$

x	y
−2	
−1	
0	
1	
2	

3. $y = -x^2$

x	y
−2	
−1	
0	
1	
2	

Name _____ Date _____

%÷ Apply Skills
The Radical Sign and Evaluating Numeric Expressions

Activity 1

Solve the radicals in each expression. Remember to use the rules of PEMDAS. Be sure to consider ± symbols in your answers.

Model	$\sqrt{100 + 44} + 9$
	Answer $\sqrt{100 + 44} + 9$
	$\sqrt{144} + 9$
	$\pm 12 + 9$
	$12 + 9$ and $-12 + 9$
	21 or -3

1. $\sqrt{24 + 12}$ _____

2. $\sqrt{56 + 8}$ _____

3. $\sqrt{86 - 5} + 2$ _____

4. $3 \cdot \sqrt{37 + 12}$ _____

5. $2 \cdot \sqrt{4 + 5} + 5$ _____

Name _____ Date _____

Problem-Solving Activity
Changing the Shape of a Non-Linear Function

Activity 1

Create a table and graph for the functions $y = -\frac{1}{2}x^2$ and $y = -2x^2$. After
you create the tables and the graphs, answer the questions.

$y = -\frac{1}{2}x^2$

x	y
−3	
−2	
−1	
0	
1	
2	
3	

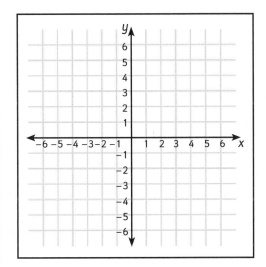

$y = -2x^2$

x	y
−3	
−2	
−1	
0	
1	
2	
3	

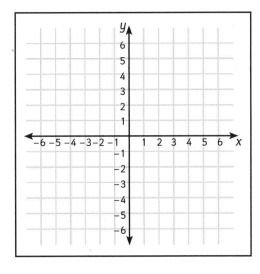

Name _____ Date _____

1. How are the tables different for the two functions?

   _____

   _____

   _____

2. How are the graphs different for the two functions?

   _____

   _____

   _____

3. Explain the impact of a negative coefficient on a parabola. Explain the impact of different-sized negative coefficients on a parabola.

   _____

   _____

   _____

   _____

mBook **Reinforce Understanding**
Use the mBook *Study Guide* to review lesson concepts.

Name _____ Date _____

 ## Skills Maintenance
Squaring Numbers

Activity 1

Square each of the numbers. You may use a calculator.

1. 2^2 _____

2. 1.2^2 _____

3. $\left(\dfrac{1}{2}\right)^2$ _____

4. $(4 + 2)^2$ _____

5. 2.8^2 _____

Unit 10

Name _____ Date _____

%÷ Apply Skills
The Radical Sign and Algebraic Equations

Activity 1

Use algebra and properties of square roots to solve the each expression.

Model

$\sqrt{x+3} = 6$ ___x = 33___

Answer: $\left(\sqrt{x+3}\right)^2 = 6^2$ Square both sides.

$\quad\quad x + 3 = 36$ Remove the radical on the left.

$\quad\quad x = 33$ Solve.

Check the answer: $\sqrt{33 + 3} = 6$

$\quad\quad\quad\quad\quad\quad\quad\quad \sqrt{36} = 6$ TRUE

1. $\sqrt{x+2} = 4$ _____

   Show your work here.

2. $\sqrt{2x+2} = 2$ _____

   Show your work here.

3. $\sqrt{4x-1} = 1$ _____

   Show your work here.

4. $\sqrt{x-3} = 3$ _____

   Show your work here.

5. $\sqrt{14+2} = x$ _____

   Show your work here.

Name _____ Date _____

Problem-Solving Activity
Other Non-Linear Functions

**Match the function with the correct graph and circle the answer.
Write a sentence explaining your answer.**

1. Circle the graph for this function $y = 3x^2$.

(a)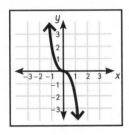

(b)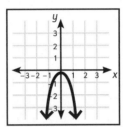

(c)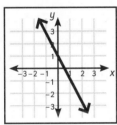

(d)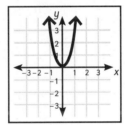

_____

_____

2. Circle the graph for this function $y = -2x^2$.

(a)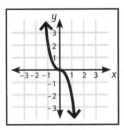

(b)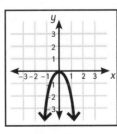

(c)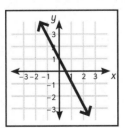

(d)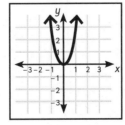

_____

_____

Unit 10

Name _____ Date _____

Skills Maintenance
Solving Square Roots

Activity 1

Use a calculator to solve the square roots. Round your answers to the nearest tenth.

1. $\sqrt{32}$ ± _____

2. $\sqrt{48}$ ± _____

3. $\sqrt{62}$ ± _____

4. $\sqrt{80}$ ± _____

5. $\sqrt{99}$ ± _____

Name _____ Date _____

%÷ Apply Skills
Using Number Sense With Square Roots

Activity 1

Estimate the square roots. Use perfect squares to narrow down the location between two whole numbers. Compute the multiplication and square root on a calculator and compare them to find your estimate.

1. Estimate $\sqrt{32}$. It is between $\sqrt{}$ and $\sqrt{}$. Put the numbers on the number line:

    $\longleftarrow\!\longrightarrow$

    What is your estimate for $\sqrt{32}$?

    _____

    Compute the square root on a calculator and compare. _____

2. Estimate $\sqrt{51}$. It is between $\sqrt{}$ and $\sqrt{}$. Put the numbers on the number line:

    $\longleftarrow\!\longrightarrow$

    What is your estimate for $\sqrt{51}$? _____

    Compute the square root on a calculator and compare. _____

3. Estimate $\sqrt{12}$. It is between $\sqrt{}$ and $\sqrt{}$. Put the numbers on the number line:

    $\longleftarrow\!\longrightarrow$

    What is your estimate for $\sqrt{12}$? _____

    Compute the square root on a calculator and compare. _____

4. Estimate $\sqrt{80}$. It is between $\sqrt{}$ and $\sqrt{}$. Put the numbers on the number line:

    $\longleftarrow\!\longrightarrow$

    What is your estimate for $\sqrt{80}$? _____

    Compute the square root on a calculator and compare. _____

Unit 10

Name _____ Date _____

 ## Skills Maintenance
Exponents and Repeated Multiplication

Activity 1

Rewrite each of the problems with exponents as repeated multiplication.
Then use your calculator to solve.

Model	2^5 $\underline{2 \cdot 2 \cdot 2 \cdot 2 \cdot 2 = 32}$

1. 3^4 _____

2. 4^2 _____

3. 5^3 _____

4. 2^6 _____

5. 1^9 _____

Name _____ Date _____

Unit Review
Square Roots and Irrational Numbers

Activity 1

Use a calculator to find the square roots for the numbers in the table.
Round your answer to the nearest hundredth.

Number	Square Roots
20	
32	
45	
61	

Activity 2

Solve the equations with square roots. Remember that anything to the 0
power is 1.

1. $2^2 + 2^3$ _____

2. 3^0 _____

3. $4^2 + 4^2$ _____

4. $3^0 + 2^2$ _____

5. $2^0 + 2^3$ _____

6. $100^0 + 2^2$ _____

7. $2^2 + 5^0$ _____

8. $3^2 + 3^0$ _____

Activity 3

Find the value of x.

1. $\sqrt{3 + x} = 4$ $x =$ _____

2. $x^2 = 64$ $x =$ _____

3. $x^2 + 9 = 25$ $x =$ _____

4. $\sqrt{4x} = 8$ $x =$ _____

5. $2x^2 = 50$ $x =$ _____

Name _____ Date _____

Activity 4

Use what you know about square numbers to estimate the number in each problem. Use the number line to show how you figured out your answer.

1. $\sqrt{20}$

   Show the perfect square numbers around 20 and where $\sqrt{20}$ would be on the number line.

   <--->

   What is your estimated answer of $\sqrt{20}$? _____

2. $\sqrt{27}$

   Show the perfect square numbers around 27 and where $\sqrt{27}$ would be on the number line.

   <--->

   What is your estimated answer of $\sqrt{27}$? _____

3. $\sqrt{35}$

   Show the perfect square numbers around 35 and where $\sqrt{35}$ would be on the number line.

   <--->

   What is your estimated answer of $\sqrt{35}$? _____

Name _____ Date _____

Activity 5

Find the missing side length for each of the right triangles using the Pythagorean Theorem. Round to the hundredth.

1. What is the length of side *a?* _____

    Show your work here.

    $a = ?$ $c = 7$ $b = 6$

2. What is the length of side *b?* _____

    Show your work here.

    $b = ?$ $a = 9$ $c = 10$

3. What is the length of side *c?* _____

    Show your work here.

    $a = 10$ c $b = 5$

4. What is the length of side *c?* _____

    c $a = 7$ $b = 5$

5. What is the length of side *a?* _____

    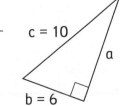
    $c = 10$ a $b = 6$

Unit 10

Name _____ Date _____

Unit Review
Non-Linear Functions

Activity 1

For each of the *x/y* tables, write the linear function using an equation. Then graph the function.

1.

x	y
1	3
2	6
3	9
4	12
5	15

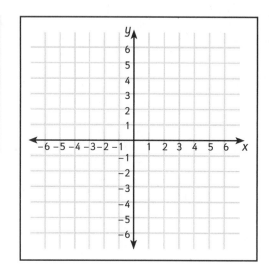

What is the function? _____

2.

x	y
1	4
2	8
3	12
4	16
5	20

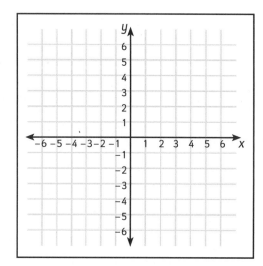

What is the function? _____